Pelican Book A807

Style and Civilization | *Edited by John Fleming and Hugh Honour*

Pre-Classical by John Boardman

John Boardman, Fellow of Merton College, Oxford, and Reader in Classical Archaeology in the University of Oxford, was born in 1927. He was educated at Chigwell School and Magdalene College, Cambridge, then went to Athens as Student and later Assistant Director (1952–5) of the British School at Athens. From 1955 to 1959 he was Assistant Keeper of the Ashmolean Museum. He was elected Fellow of the Society of Antiquaries in 1957, received the Cromer Greek Prize in 1959, and has been a Corresponding Member of the German Archaeological Institute since 1961. He has travelled widely in Greek lands and excavated in Smyrna, Knossos, Chios, and Libya; his main interest being in the art and archaeology of archaic Greece and their relationship to the history of that period. His previous publications include *The Cretan Collection in Oxford, Island Gems, The Date of the Knossos Tablets, The Greeks Overseas* (Pelican), *Greek Art*, and various articles on the archaeology of archaic Greece. He has served as editor of the *Journal of Hellenic Studies*. John Boardman is married, with two children.

John Boardman

Style and Civilization

Pre-Classical

From Crete to Archaic Greece

With 104 illustrations

Penguin Books

Penguin Books Ltd, Harmondsworth,
Middlesex, England
Penguin Books Inc., 3300 Clipper Mill Road,
Baltimore 11, Md, U.S.A.
Penguin Books Australia Ltd, Ringwood,
Victoria, Australia

First published 1967
Copyright © John Boardman, 1967

Designed by Gerald Cinamon
Made and printed in Great Britain by
Balding and Mansell, London and Wisbech
Set in Monotype Garamond

Contents

Editorial Foreword

The series to which this book belongs is devoted to both the history and the problems of style in European art. It is expository rather than critical. The aim is to discuss each important style in relation to contemporary shifts in emphasis and direction both in the other, non-visual arts and in thought and civilization as a whole. In this first volume of the series, however, the very limited and fragmentary nature of the surviving evidence has necessarily limited the author's scope – our knowledge of the civilization of early Greece being drawn almost exclusively from its visual remains.

The series is intended for the general reader but it is written at a level which should interest the specialist as well. Beyond this there has been no attempt at uniformity. Each author has had complete liberty in his mode of treatment and has been free to be as selective as he wished. For selection and compression are inevitable in a series, such as this, whose scope extends beyond the history of art.

Preface

There was no abrupt transition from the world of pre-classical Greek art to the classical. These are terms of convenience only, and in many ways there is less in the history of art to mark the passage from what is described in this volume to what is described in the next than there is to distinguish these first chapters one from the other. But by the beginning of the fifth century B.C., where our break is made, Greek art had absorbed and adopted all that it needed from other and older civilizations, and was already approaching maturity. What of the brilliant Bronze Age past of Greece had not been forgotten, had by now been assimilated, like the Heroic tradition celebrated by the Homeric poets; while in Europe and Italy other artistic traditions, each influenced in varying degrees by Greece, had already been established and were in due course to play their part in the development of what we call western art.

Prehistoric Greece, the Bronze Age palaces of Crete and the Mycenaean Empire, have to be considered here for the simple reason that they existed, and not because of any profound effect they had on the later development of Greek art. But it is of no little interest to historians, both of art and of society, to see how much and how little the achievements of a civilization can survive a Dark Age of some two or three centuries, and how they may be seen reflected in what is to all appearances a fresh start by the same peoples in the same lands.

Throughout this book we shall be dealing with objects which have a significance far beyond what we can now read into them about the artistic tastes and talents of their day. We are dealing with prehistory and proto-history, when contemporary records are virtually non-existent, and when it is from their artefacts alone that we can hope to learn anything about the history, society and religion of the peoples who made them. So it has become the archaeologist's preserve, and what to many may stand in its own right as a work of art, to him may also be evidence which can date a building, attest a trade route, identify a deity or a migrating people. It is impossible, of course, to divorce the interests. More than in most other periods the objects can claim significance as works of art mainly through their context, their date, their relationship to more mature or more primitive attempts at the same thing.

It becomes, therefore, a comparatively easy matter to describe pre-classical art in terms of the societies which produced it, because as often as not it is our only evidence for the nature of those societies. We would know plenty about Renaissance Italy without its pictures. We would know nothing about Minoan, Mycenaean or Geometric Greece without their surviving works of art or handicraft. But there is serious danger too. Modern interpretations of the arts – about what is 'decadent', 'derivative', 'original' – may easily colour reconstructions of ancient history and life. And we may be misled by an age in which art is a professional matter into attaching the wrong sort of importance to what may be the works of intelligent and sensitive craftsmen rather than of sophisticated artists.

In these chapters it will be convenient to sketch a little of what can be known about the contemporary society before the development of its art is described. It is very largely a story of 'development' too: the observation of how foreign influences and native talent can combine to produce new forms, rarely of how the talent of one man or a group can be felt. We will never be able to pick on a single work or series of works and say 'this is the essence of Minoan, or Geometric, or Archaic Greek art', because the essence is one of progress and change, of new problems faced, solved, or given up in despair.

Another thing which makes study of the pre-classical period different from that of almost any other period of western art, is that it is one which saw the gradual discovery of what may now seem quite basic techniques and conventions. Thus, there was a time when the only tool with which to work marble was emery; a time when it was impossible to cast a bronze figure more than about a foot high, and a time when the artist simply had not discovered how to render a proper three-quarter view, let alone perspective. So the story becomes one of progressive discovery, and by the end of our period we shall find that most of the basic techniques had been learnt and that the artist was well on his way to a fully realistic, representational art. There were certainly later periods in which some of the techniques had to be re-learnt, and of course time and again the artist hit on new ways of representing the old, familiar subjects – new ways which more fully satisfied his age and temperament. But inevitably the study of any period of art in which the changes are being rung – albeit in novel ways – on the old subjects and techniques is going to differ considerably from a study of the period in which those techniques and subjects were for the first time mastered.

Finally it should be remarked that virtually all that is described in this book has been discovered in the last hundred years. These arts of early Greece are fundamental to the proper study of classical art, yet were almost completely unknown to the Roman and Renaissance artists whose works represent the continuance of the 'classical tradition' in the west. Many of the principles of classical Greek art and of what went before it are foreign to this tradition and it is possible to misunderstand them through over-familiarity with the variety of what has followed. In the history of art, as in any narrative, it is as well to begin at the beginning.

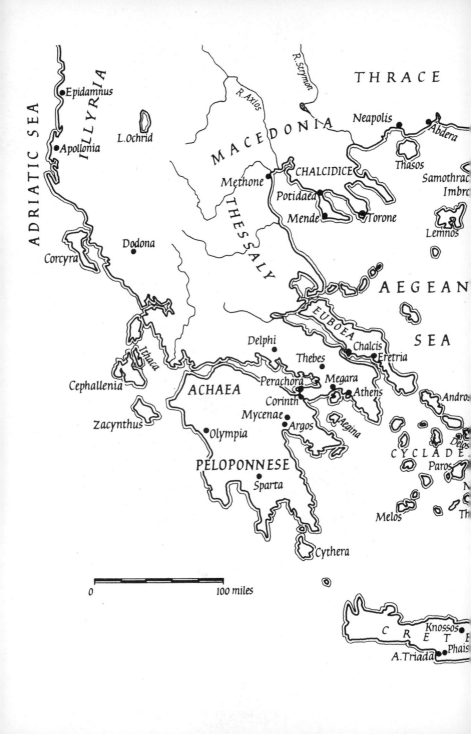

Pre-Classical

1. Figure of a woman. About 3000 B.C. (Clay)

I

Minoans and Mycenaeans

Greece became the cradle of western civilization very largely because of its geographical position. It enjoyed an almost perfect climate, warm and temperate; the land was difficult to farm and gave short shrift to indolence, but it rewarded hard work; the long coastline and myriad islands encouraged seafaring and stimulated a lively curiosity; and it was within reasonably easy reach of the other, older civilizations of the Near East and Egypt, so that it could learn from them without becoming too deeply involved in their troubles.

The two great valley civilizations of the Nile and Mesopotamia were linked by the 'fertile crescent' of land, part of which formed the seaboard of the Eastern Mediterranean and gave access to Cyprus, the Aegean and Greece. The character of these civilizations is largely reflected in their arts – hieratic, highly conventional, slow to develop, for all their technical accomplishment, and rarely illumined by those flashes of insight or individual brilliance which rivet our attention so frequently in Greek art, even from the earliest times. Greece and her islands were settled first from the east and their arts were an extension of eastern styles, tempered by the peculiar quality with which the Aegean seems to touch everything that has its origin there. Naturally enough, some features of early Greek art and society share certain, usually not very striking or important, characteristics with those of the east and Egypt. But this only serves to accentuate the contrast with the later Greek achievement and gives us more readily a standard by which to judge it, for it is fair to say that the arts of the east and Egypt provided a reservoir of inspiration without which classical Greek art might never have taken quite the form which it did.

The art of primitive peoples is very largely conditioned by the materials and tools available to them. They are least hampered by such technical and other limitations when working with clay and thus it is the clay figurines of Stone Age

2. Figure of a woman. About 3000 B.C.

Greece which appeal to us most directly today. Most are of women, of a type current in many parts of the ancient world. In Greece some are unusually modelled, with comparatively slim and natural proportions, like the remarkable neolithic figure found at Lerna in 1956 [1]. The majority, however, have the gross, squat bodies, with big breasts and buttocks, of the universal mother, or, as some would have her, mother goddess.

As Greece emerged from the Stone Age and began to accept the new crafts and way of life which went with the working of metal, it is on the islands that we can observe the most notable signs of some artistic activity. It was in some ways natural that Crete and the islands of the Aegean Sea should take a prominent part in dealings overseas and that it would be the cities of mainland Greece that would develop and consolidate what they had learned. The islands' importance was enhanced by the fact that among them lay the source of obsidian – volcanic glass which can be split into blades of razor sharpness and was in demand even far beyond the Aegean.

On the islands a different material suggested a different form for the old neolithic goddess figures. Fine white marble was to be had without quarrying on several of the Cyclades – the group of islands that lie just north of Crete, strung out like stepping-stones across the Aegean. Though difficult to work without metal tools this beautiful material could be smoothed and cut with pebbles and blades of emery; and emery, too, was to be found on one of the islands. The figurines betray the technique clearly [2]. Smooth surface planes intersect with sharp angles, and even the more fully rounded figures still follow the convention established for the typical Cycladic head – flat-topped with a long streamlined nose. It is little wonder that modern artists, like Brancusi and Modigliani, should have admired and sought inspiration in these early figures; but they should be judged with knowledge of the limitations of technique and material and by comparison with contemporary work in other materials, notably clay. The stone figures have been found in tombs, but it is not known whether they represent goddesses, wives or concubines. Some are male, some even play musical instruments.

In the humbler craft of the potter, to which we shall often have to turn in this book because his products are more often and better preserved than any other pre-classical Greek artefacts, decoration is generally very simple. It had not always been so, and in parts of Greece, especially to the north where there were flourishing Stone Age communities, there was pottery decorated in a most eccentric and lively abstract manner, such as was never to be seen again in Greece.

But all these – the Cycladic figurines, the Stone Age pottery of Thessaly – are in a way foreign to the main development of Greek Bronze Age art. Indeed they are almost as far from our theme as the cave paintings of Lascaux or Altamira. Nevertheless, they introduce us to what was happening in the Aegean world in the years before the great Bronze Age palaces – and they introduce us to pottery and white marble, the two media in which, many centuries later, the Greeks were to make their first essays in painting and monumental sculpture.

Early in the second millennium B.C. Greece and the islands suffered a convulsive and epoch-making invasion. Into the mainland of Greece came the first Greek-speakers: and to the island of Crete a race – not Greek – which was to develop a civilization of a highly individual character and quality which only very remotely reflects the eastern origins of its people.

Sir Arthur Evans christened the civilization which he revealed at Knossos 'Minoan', after the legendary king of that city. He had discovered a vast, rich and well-preserved palace site, and Minoan art first became known as the art of the Palace of Minos at Knossos. This, as it turned out, was wholly just, for Minoan art is essentially palatial. The finest objects are from the palaces, villas and royal cemeteries, and hardly ever from towns or isolated cult places. From what we can judge it seems that Crete was administered from a limited number of palace centres (Knossos, Mallia, Phaistos) and these, especially Knossos, were the artistic as well as the administrative foci.

In the first period of Minoan art – the period of the Early Palaces (about 1900–1600 B.C.) – it is the pottery which tells most about current taste. The use of the fast wheel had by now been learned from the east, and the palace potteries were soon turning out fine vases, whose exceptionally thin walls have earned for some of them the title 'eggshell ware'. Their shapes are often fussy, with crinkly rims and the sort of trivial embellishments which might seem to derive from metalwork but which in fact come as readily to a craftsman with pliant clay in his fingers. Apart from their tendency to have the centre of gravity set rather high there is little in the shapes of Minoan vases to impress us. Some of the more flamboyant examples have been found in recent years at Phaistos [3].

The vases were painted black and the decoration, picked out in white and various shades of red, is almost always abstract. Animal or recognizable floral motifs are so rare that they can almost be counted on the fingers of one hand.

The patterns themselves generally obey the principle that a single motif is developed or repeated all over the surface of the vase, or at least on its two sides. This seems a logical enough way to paint a vase, but we shall see that it stands in marked contrast with what was subsequently to be preferred by Greeks both in the Bronze Age and in later times. For we must remember that although Minoan art is, as it were, the mainspring of Mycenaean Greek art, still the Minoans were not themselves Greeks or even Greek-speakers. The most elaborate examples of this principle of decoration involve twisting, interlocking or radial subjects, such as are seen also on other Cretan works of this period.

While the best of the painted pottery was found on the palace sites it was of course also current elsewhere and the tombs and houses of humbler folk were furnished with pottery decorated in the same manner. The other decorative arts by which we know Minoan Crete are, as might be expected, more restricted in their application.

The palaces themselves were rambling structures, with groups of small rooms, magazines and apartments set round a central courtyard. It seems that Minoan architecture had little feeling for the impressive façade or the sort of unity of plan which was so well expressed in later Greek times, and can be observed to some degree even in Mycenaean Greece. The Minoan palaces housed their royal families and priests, but also served as administrative headquarters in which the tribute or tax due from the royal estates was accounted and in or near which the royal stores were housed. We think first, of course, of the great magazines of oil jars in the palaces, but there were stores for equipment and foodstuffs too, of which we learn only from the accounts kept on clay tablets. The palaces served also to house artists' workshops. There were big pottery stores in both the Minoan and Mycenaean palaces and there can be no doubt that the potteries themselves were near at hand. At Knossos there is evidence for the presence of ivory-workers, seal-engravers and other craftsmen. The finest of their products were naturally for the adornment of the palace or for the use and enjoyment of royalty and officials. It is to these finer, palatial products of the Early Palaces that we

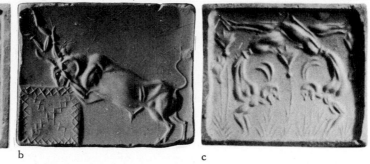

a   b   c

now turn. We shall find on them richer and more ambitious decoration, especially of human figures and animals, than on any surviving vases.

Perhaps the most important of these 'luxury goods' of the Early Palace period are the engraved seals. They were used for sealing boxes or the stoppers of vases and, no doubt, documents, with wax or clay. Since their usage was principally involved with 'big business' they were carved with a style and elegance suitable to the rank of their owners. That they were, or became, more generally used is shown by finds in commoners' tombs, and there is one whole class which seems never to have been used for sealing but to have served some amuletic purpose. It was, in fact, these fine stones which first brought Evans to Crete. He found them still worn as amulets – or 'milk-stones' as they were called – by nursing mothers in the peasant villages.

These early seals are three-sided prisms worn like beads, or small stamp seals, but later the more popular shapes were developed – the circular lentoid seals (lens-shaped) and the almond-shaped 'amygdaloid' seals, which could be worn on a necklace or slung at the wrist. The best were cut in hard, semi-precious stones – agates or chalcedonies. The earliest prisms carry devices which seem to portray industry or husbandry. Others have devices which are related to the hieroglyphic script used for a while in Crete, but the individual characters are often elaborated, or they are varied by the introduction of pseudo-hieroglyphs – often studies of animals or animal-heads executed with a lively understanding of natural form and a real appreciation of the way it can be translated into pure pattern. A good example is shown here [4a] – cats' heads with headlamp eyes. Other seals again carry the torsional subjects related to those seen on painted vases; and towards the end of the period of the Early Palaces there are more ambitious animal studies, like that of the youth leaping on to a bull while it drinks at a tank [4b]. Of the same date are the acrobats doing handstands in a field of lilies [4c].

In these seals we are given our first opportunity to observe the Minoan artist's treatment of animals and, occasionally, human beings. There was always to be something rather 'impressionistic' (in the more hackneyed sense of the word) about it. In the Near East and Egypt the conventions for the representation of animals and human figures had almost reduced them to abstract patterns, severely restricting the variety of poses and gestures which could be portrayed. And to some extent, especially in the Geometric period, Greek artists were to be subject to similar conventions, of course self-imposed and unconscious. But the Minoans knew no such inhibitions. Hardly any two of their finer animal studies are quite alike. Instead of the stereotyped, schematized Egyptian cats and birds, we get lively impressions of animals in characteristic or striking poses. They are not by any means detailed anatomical studies, but the artist has fastened on particular features which he allows to dominate his composition – the sweeping horns of a goat, the powerful neck and shoulders of a bull [4b], or the fleetness of foot of various beasts shown with their fore- and hind-legs at full stretch in a 'flying gallop'. Some of the earliest examples of the gallop motif appear on the seal-stones of the Early Palace period though one example shown here [21] is of later date.

The seals were sometimes cut to give impressions in especially high relief, but they offer nothing like the sort of miniature sculptural style which appears on Archaic Greek gems. The cutting and detail are rather more deliberately suited to the size and shape of the stone. Indeed we look in vain for anything monumental, sculptural or otherwise, in Minoan art.

This is readily seen if we consider surviving works in the round. There are none even approaching life size. The clay figurines found in the Cretan sanctuaries are small and very roughly modelled with no real attention to detail or features: the animals betray nothing of that verve which the seal-engraver could convey on his tiny stones. But the bronze-worker offers us something a little better. The models from which he took his moulds were made of clay or wax, but they were executed with greater care than the clay figurines.

5. Worshipper or 'flute-player'. 1700–1600 B.C. (Bronze)

Bronze animal figures are generally of little merit, but the human figures – worshippers saluting the deity, or an unusual flute-player [5] – are a very different matter. The men stand stiffly to attention but the supple curve of back and thigh lends them real grace. Anatomy and proportions are ignored or distorted, but distorted to effect; and no attempt is made to represent details of features or limbs, let alone facial expression. The bronze is left without smoothing or polishing, with the rough plastic surface which its clay or wax model originally bore when it left the artist's hands. This is a degree of impressionism which may seem out of keeping with the miniaturist precision of the contemporary seal-engraver, but in fact it reflects the same deliberate choice of what seems expressive, at the expense of all else.

The female figures show worshippers in the full-flounced skirts worn by Minoan women, and the tight bodice which left the heavy breasts bare. The head of the figure illustrated [6] is bared, almost featureless, but here the artist is excited more by the snake-like tangle of locks which collect over the nape of the neck and shoulders. Bronzes such as this are far more typical of the best and most sensitive work of Minoan artists than the more familiar and popular faience figures of the 'snake-goddess' and her attendant which are so often illustrated. The main interest in these garish figures lies in the colour and detail preserved in the glaze which covers them. The body of the figurines is made of a silica composition: an Egyptian technique, miscalled faience. The snake-goddess is dressed as the bronzes, with flounced skirt and bared breasts, but, apart from the generous proportions of the latter, there is no serious attempt either at modelling of the body or at the poise and presence which inform the bronzes.

In all this the influence of foreign arts is barely perceptible. Yet they had their effect, in some fields. Egyptian stone vases inspired a number of superb works in Crete where there were rich deposits of finely veined and coloured stones. These were carved with an eye to the visual effect of the veining of the finished surface [7], and the patterns of variegated stones were often copied in other arts. In jewellery too, Egypt or the Near East must have inspired much of the gold work of the Early Palaces. Some of the finest comes from the royal cemetery at Mallia. One piece, probably from this site, has a very Egyptian scene of a prince, wearing the Egyptian feather crown and foreign disk ear-rings, and standing like Pharaoh on a Nile

6. Figure of a woman. 1700–1600 B.C. (Bronze)

7. Two jugs. About 2000 B.C.

boat [8]. But the other features are Minoan, and the superb hornets pendant from Mallia [9] shows a completely Minoan composition, even though executed in the filigree and granulation technique learnt from Egypt.

Finally there are the frescoes, a wholly palatial art. There is still some doubt about which may be attributed to the period of the Early Palace at Knossos, but it seems possible that the so-called Miniature Frescoes belong there, and they display some of the impressionistic effects which we have seen to be a striking feature of the seals and bronzes. The frescoes represent crowds watching some religious spectacle or athletic event in the palace grounds. The massed heads are flicked in with blobs of colour in a most direct and simple manner – red for the men, white for the women. Where a little more detail is admitted, as on some of the larger figures, the artist depicts animated features and gestures [10]. From the scraps that survive it is clear that the complete works were no great monumental wall-paintings. The wide patches of different colours which served as background to the pictures could not have helped the eye to pick out the significance of the individual scenes and figures. These were evidently intended to be enjoyed in detail, like panel pictures, and not all together as in a great homogeneous composition.

The sixteenth century B.C. saw the end of the Early Palaces and the beginning of the period of the New Palaces. We need not dwell on the historical problems about what provoked the change – whether the disasters were natural or man-made. Culturally there is no real break. These are the same people

8. Pendant. 1700–1600 B.C. (Gold)

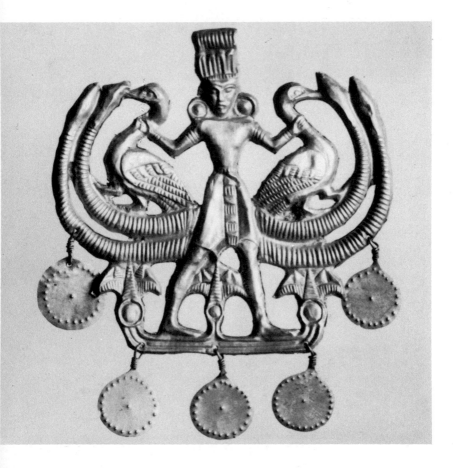

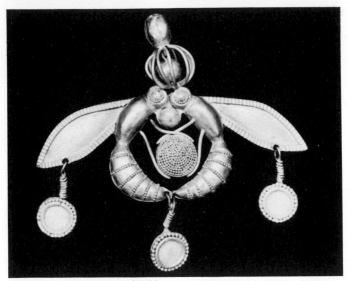

9. Pendant. 1700–1600 B.C. (Gold)

and their art developed naturally, or at least without abrupt transition, from that of earlier times. But a new people has also entered upon the scene: Greek-speakers – Mycenaeans.

The art history of the last period of the Bronze Age in the Greek world resolves itself into three stages, each distinctive in its content and significance. First, the flowering of the New Palaces of Crete in years when Mycenaeans were only beginning to admire Minoan art and copy it. Then, a generation or two in which Mycenaean control of Knossos fuses the Minoan tradition with a Greek-Mycenaean way of looking at things (for it cannot at this stage be called a developed artistic tradition). And the last stage, when Mycenae was dominant, Crete exhausted, and the Mycenaean element gained the upper hand in the development of art in Greek lands.

This is the first introduction of Greeks to our story, and it is important to see just how much the content of Mycenaean Greek art owes to the example of Minoan Crete. Until the sixteenth century B.C. the Greeks of the mainland were unsophisticated and only at those few points where direct overseas contacts could be made and maintained, did they admit the arts of Crete. Their pots were barely decorated at all. There

10. Miniature fresco. 1700–1600 B.C.

were no frescoes, jewellery or palaces in the Minoan manner. But in the sixteenth century the royal burials at Mycenae began to be furnished with Cretan works, and a new age was heralded.

The New Palace period in Crete saw the artists turning away from the imaginative abstract patterns which we have seen best deployed in earlier days on painted pottery, to a more developed interest in realism and the figurative arts. They do not, however, appear to have pursued realism for its own sake, but they seized on such natural and representational motifs as plants and marine life (shells, octopuses) as could be used for the type of all-over decoration which was favoured on the older vases.

Thus it is again the pottery which betrays the new interest most clearly. Shapes acquired a new elegance, shorn of the vulgar excrescences and plastic additions which deformed so many of the more elaborate vases of the Old Palace period. For the new subjects of decoration a new technique was adopted and the old practice of picking out the pattern in red and white on a black background [3] was replaced by more direct and natural dark-on-light painting [11 and 12].

11. Beaked jug with grasses. 1600–1500 B.C.

12. Octopus flask. About 1500 B.C.

The floral vases show us grasses tangling gracefully over the walls of a jug, unimpeded by subsidiary decoration except for the rocky ground-line from which they rise [11]. On other vases the old abstract patterns are worked out in coiled branches and over-all networks of spirals and leaves. Beside these patterns which are developed over the whole available surface of the vase we also begin to find more frequent use of floral friezes, especially at the shoulder or widest part of the vase, lending a horizontal emphasis which had been generally lacking hitherto.

No less successful was the so-called Marine Style. The serpentine tentacles of an octopus wind erratically around the vase [12] while the background is filled with rocks and sea-weed, or sometimes a variety of shells. The same shells appear in a more stylized form in friezes, like the floral bands or rows of ivy leaves and spirals.

Similar subjects and style of decoration are found on a new class of vases, carved from a soft black serpentine (generally miscalled steatite). These are either covered with the familiar octopus-and-rock pattern, or else have friezes with human figures, such as were still excluded by the vase painter. A fine example of this type is the famous Harvesters' Vase [13] which was found in one of the smaller palatial buildings in Crete, at Hagia Triada, a dependency of the Palace at Phaistos. It shows a procession of farm-workers carrying winnowing forks, accompanied by singers and a man shaking a rattle (the Egyptian *sistrum*). The upper parts of the bodies are shown in

13. The Harvesters' Vase (rhyton). 1600–1500 B.C. (Stone)

frontal view, the rest in profile, but not because the artist could not deal with a true profile. Muscles and limbs are carved boldly, yet not realistically. The tight waists, loincloths and codpieces render the conventional Minoan physique and dress, but the artist is not bound by these conventions, and the man with the rattle is individualized – a plump, sinewy rascal, rendered in true profile, with the pattern of his ribs on his side accurately observed. His and his fellow singers' mouths are shown as thick crescents of lip, and this little group of four offers as economical an expression of bellowing song and clatter as one could wish. Its almost casual naturalism and command of foreshortening can readily be appreciated today. Too readily and without due reflection, perhaps, because it is in works like these that Crete offers us something which is central to the tradition of western art – call it 'humanity', 'the common touch' or what you will – but which we seek in vain in the arts of Egypt and the east where humour goes no further than parody and the everyday is treated in terms of banal convention. If the Harvesters' Vase shows a religious procession, as it may, it is certainly not its otherworldly purpose that the artist sought to portray but simply the vivid reality of shouting, singing men.

In the seal-stones the full range of treatment of these new subjects is best seen. Human beings and monsters [14a] or elaborate and carefully modelled animals are now more often represented, in compositions which are successfully adapted to the difficult circular or oval field. The twisted bodies of the

14. Impressions of seals. 1500–1400 B.C.

a   b

creatures on many of these seals [14b] are among the most effective, and at the same time they express the old Minoan feeling for torsion and for spreading designs which own no top or bottom or sides. But these contorted animals are not simply essays in the grotesque, as they are often described, but the artist's rendering of a novel but natural viewpoint, top three-quarter of a reclining animal with his legs before him, his hindquarters twisted to one side.

Crete received ivory from Egypt or the Near East quite early in the Bronze Age, and used it for some seals. Only later did the artists attempt to carve elaborate figures in the round from the precious material. The results are of course more precise than the roughly finished bronzes. There are scraps from Knossos of large statuettes, made of several pieces dowelled together, on which details of veins and muscles can be seen to have been carved with extreme care even if not always with absolute attention to anatomical accuracy.

In the frescoes, which reflect most closely the taste and skill of the palace artists – for they are to be found only in palaces (and not all of these) and royal villas – we find the fullest expression of all the new fashions in choice of subject and style. They depict figures, often more than life size, lining the dimly lit corridors of the palace, brightening apartments or flanking halls and entrances. There is something hieratic and stilted in their poise; they lack altogether the lighter, more individual approach which the artist shows in minor works, like the Harvesters' Vase. Where there are floral patterns we find sprays of lilies, rather formally set in the manner of the succeeding period; but also lighter sketches of blossoms and shrubs, often as a landscape background to scenes with animals. The impressionistic effect was no doubt helped by the technique, for the paint had to be applied to the plaster while it was damp, and this probably helped stifle the sort of over-elaboration which is the mural painter's most serious enemy. Animal scenes are bright and original: partridges [15] and

15. Fresco with partridges. About 1500 B.C.

16. Cup: the capture of bulls. About 1500 B.C. (Gold)

hoopoes, monkeys in a garden, a cat stalking a pheasant. The colours are brilliant, and in places a sculptural effect is given by rendering figures in relief.

Such was the art of Crete in the years when the Mycenaean Greeks first took a close interest in the island; or, more probably, had been awakened to its wealth and resources by visiting Cretan merchants and by the Cretan colonies and trading posts established in the islands. In the royal Shaft Graves which Schliemann excavated at Mycenae in 1876, and in the new circle of graves found only after the last war, Cretan works of art are found beside vases and other works wholly in the mainland Greek style. So we are faced, first of all, with the problem of distinguishing between imports from Crete itself, works by Cretans employed in Greece by the Mycenaean kings, and works by Mycenaean artists in the Cretan style. Many of the gold signet rings, with their precisely cut cult-scenes, seem wholly Cretan both in their execution and the content of their devices. Cretan too, no doubt, the metal vases of such excellence as the well-known gold cups from Vaphio with their relief scenes of bull-hunting [16], or the cup with octopuses and fish from Midea [17], executed in the Cretan Marine Style. The bulls on the Vaphio cups are, like all Cretan bulls [18], almost benign, graceful creatures, singularly unsinister even when they leap among vaulting acrobats. The Cretans, and Mycenaeans, could do without the parade of horrific monsters that haunt Near Eastern and Egyptian art. What they borrowed they tamed. What they invented was decorative and innocuous. This is a characteristic approach which we shall meet again in a much later period of Greek art.

As well as the gold vases and signet rings found in Greece there are other works which appear to be executed in a wholly Cretan style and yet are in an unfamiliar technique, or which portray subjects that the Cretans seem to have avoided. Notable among these are works which involve inlays of

17. Cup: octopuses. About 1500 B.C. (Gold)

18. Bull's head (rhyton). About 1500 B.C. (Stone)

precious metal in bronze. The best known are the daggers from Mycenae, on whose bronze blades are inlaid figures cut out of sheet silver and gold and set in a background of black *niello*. Some of the scenes on these, and on similar daggers from other royal Mycenaean graves, are wholly Minoan – the cats chasing ducks beside a river [19], linked spiral patterns, shells and foliage. But others, like the great lion hunt, show scenes quite foreign to the Minoan artist's repertoire. Other examples of inlaid metal work of a kind still not found in Crete are the silver vessels, from Mycenae and elsewhere, inlaid with gold flowers or human heads. When we meet this type of work in Greece we may well suppose that Cretan craftsmen had been installed in the Mycenaean citadels to work in their traditional style, but with new subjects and new techniques.

Another notable difference between these finds in Greece which are so Minoan in style, and the finds in Crete itself, is the use of precious metals. In Crete only two or three rather simple cups of gold and silver have been found. Mycenae had access to gold which was, it seems, denied to Crete. How she won it is not known, but it afforded a rich new field for the Cretan artists employed by the Mycenaean kings. The gold cups from Vaphio and Midea, which have already been mentioned, are wholly Minoan and seem the work of Cretans, yet

19. Dagger blade: cats hunting ducks. About 1500 B.C. (Inlaid bronze)

20. Disk. About 1500 B.C. (Gold)

perhaps they too were made on the Greek mainland and not imported from Crete. Much of the gold jewellery in Mycenae is, however, decorated in a style which seems to hark back to the earlier, abstract Minoan patterns with their torsional interlocking motifs, for example the gold disks used for personal adornment and sewn on to clothing [20].

The effect of Minoan art on Mycenaean Greece is easily judged from the finds in Greece itself. But before we examine how Mycenaean and Minoan combined in Crete we should pause to consider the political and social background to this important phase in pre-classical Greek art; though we must always bear in mind that the only available evidence for an historical sketch is the objects we have been discussing – their date, style and distribution.

Crete had for long been the dominant power in the Aegean world. The island was controlled from its palace centres, and the kings were strong enough to leave their palaces unwalled, secure from threats from overseas and, it seems, from each other. Cretan ships plied the waters of the Eastern Mediterranean, to the Near East and Egypt. At Miletus, on the coast of Asia Minor, a Minoan settlement was already established in the period of the Early Palaces, and we find Minoan settlements or evidence for strong Cretan influence in many of the Greek islands and in Syria at the same early date.

The Mycenaeans were the heirs to this Minoan empire and command of the seas. They were to replace the Minoan settlements with their own, and have even more to do with the peoples who lived by the eastern waters, at least by way of trade. We have seen how their first experience of Cretan life and art seems to be marked by the import of Cretan objects and the arrival of Cretan artists who made jewellery for their kings and painted their palaces with frescoes in the Knossian style. They encouraged new techniques, like metal inlaying: but what, if anything, of their own did they add to the exotic and foreign Minoan art which they seem to have been so ready to accept?

Many scholars have attempted to isolate specifically Mycenaean elements in the hybrid Minoan-Mycenaean art of the end of the Greek Bronze Age. It is difficult, because the content of all the figurative arts was wholly and inevitably Minoan, and so it is something in the handling and treatment of the Minoan motifs which has to be sought. Something can, I think, be distinguished, although it is not easily described and the terms in which it has sometimes been discussed assume a greater knowledge of the artists of antiquity than we can honestly claim.

A principle of Minoan art had been its fondness for movement, for over-all patterns and torsion, applied to abstract and later to representational subjects, producing lively and somewhat unstable compositions. The Mycenaean principle, on the other hand, has been defined as tectonic. The lines of a composition stand vertically and horizontally, not in bold cutting diagonals or whirls and arcs. In the decorative arts this can, and did, lead to dullness and rigidity. But in figure compositions it offers the possibility of developing scenes in a way quite unknown in Minoan art. In effect it offers the possibility of a true narrative art, of a sort which seems never to have interested Crete. Or perhaps it would be nearer the truth to say that the Mycenaeans preferred a decorative narrative style which could not readily be served by the inverted or repetitive Minoan compositions.

Examples of the new manner may be seen already in the art of the Mycenae Shaft Graves, as on the bezel of a gold ring [21] carved with a stag hunt, the chariot horses stretched in a fine flying gallop, the quarry set above them in the field. But the best place in which to test this new approach to the content of Minoan art is in Crete itself, in the second half of the fifteenth century. By about the mid-century Mycenaean interest in

21. Ring: stag hunt. About 1500 B.C. (Gold)

Cretan affairs seems to have reached the point at which a Mycenaean prince was himself installed on the throne at Knossos. We cannot know how this came about. It could have been quite peacefully. By this time most of the other centres in Crete had been overthrown by the effects of the cataclysmic eruption of Thera. The Cretan script had already been adapted for the new tongue – Greek – and the administrative records found by Evans (the 'Linear B' Tablets) show that the whole island paid tribute to Knossos. This is the last major period of the palace at Knossos, and it is under a Mycenaean king. Its art was called the Palace Style by Evans, and we might hope to see in it the first results of the marriage of Minoan and Mycenaean.

We must look first, inevitably, at the pottery. The motifs of the Floral and Marine Style remained popular but the individual patterns became increasingly stylized. The flowers stand stiff, ornate and lifeless like wax lilies [22]. The sacred axe is enlisted as a decorative motif [23]. More often now the body of the vase is broken up into horizontal bands which are decorated with repetitive floral, marine or abstract devices, like spirals or patterns copying architectural mouldings. Though perhaps not immediately appealing to modern eyes, these vases are certainly impressive and their painted decoration is always bold, confident and precise. There is in fact something truly monumental about them – and this is something which can certainly not be said of the decoration of any earlier Cretan vases, even the largest.

It is more difficult to distinguish at first the Mycenaean element in the decoration of seal-stones, for there seems to have been no tradition in this craft in mainland Greece at all. Yet it is in the small figure scenes on the seals and perhaps the ring illustrated [21] that we come to see best the more tectonic, narrative compositions which can be singled out as characteristic of Mycenaean rather than Minoan taste.

The frescoes seem to tell very much the same story, although it should be admitted that it is none too easy to distinguish which are in fact the latest of the paintings which decorated the walls of Knossos. The Minoan lightness of touch and sympathy for natural forms and objects is replaced by a more rigid, stereotyped treatment of the figures. They seem now more like the cut-outs found at the back of children's comics; but they are finely drawn, and indeed the detailed rendering of the flying hair, a tense arm or leg is more impressive than the over-all composition. For now the pictures tell a story – or seem to – as though each panel or frieze were part of a strip cartoon rather than a purely decorative tableau.

In this period we observe Minoan art just past its prime, caught in a stage of incipient decadence by the new outlook of the Mycenaean Greeks, who for the rest of the Bronze Age were to experiment, to little real effect, with the Minoan models they had adopted. If, in this transitional phase, there is still much that can impress and move us, it is probably because so much still lay in the hands of Cretan artists, working either in their native island or in Greece itself. More than ever before this was a palatial art, and we are no nearer to an appreciation of the Minoans' character through their art, than we were before. It has shown a lively sense of colour and composition, an interest in natural subjects and in the representation of motion, or fleeting moments. Do we read from this that they were a volatile, sensitive people? They had no interest in narrative art, and little enough in religious (unless we cannot recognize it). Did they, then, completely lack the sort of imagination which always characterized the true Greeks? We can see something of them in their pictures. Do the bared breasts and swelling codpieces display a sexual pride? And if so, why is there not a single representation of love-making or even the mildest suggestive scene of the type that virtually every other major art and civilization of the ancient world can show, often to excess? It might seem perverse to condemn a civilization because it produced no pornography, but this lacuna remains an odd feature of the Minoan world, and one not wholly explained by any hypothetical religious interdiction or palace protocol.

In the last two centuries of the Bronze Age, 1400–1200 B.C., the Mycenaean Greeks ruled the Aegean world. Their control of Knossos had been short-lived, but Crete was to remain in the Mycenaean sphere, in a position of comparative unimportance after her lost glory, and in her arts still very much living on her past.

The Greeks had built up a bureaucratic system which may have been modelled on the Cretan palace organization. The Mycenaean centres were again palaces, but of a very different type, as befitted a very different type of people. Their nucleus was the *megaron*, a sort of baronial hall, around which were clustered the stores, workrooms and homes of retainers.

Before the main hall, with its central hearth and throne, was a court, often with a ceremonial entrance. All was enclosed within stout fortification walls such as Crete never saw, and outside them lay other houses, of the townsfolk. While the mass of the people no doubt lived the traditional agrarian life of the country, their princes had to fight for their security. They lived by the sword, and so in fear. The walls they built were against each other as much as against remoter threats of the kind which were in the end to be their downfall. Since the arts of Mycenaean Greece are, as they were in Crete, centred in the few main towns and palaces, they reflect this unsettled way of life and provide a marked contrast – in subjects at least – with the arts of the Minoan palaces. 'In subjects at least' we must say, because the stock in trade, the techniques and conventions were all taken over from Crete.

Already. in the Shaft Graves we have seen objects of apparently Cretan workmanship decorated with hunting scenes of a type alien to the Minoans. Beside them were other objects decorated in a similar manner, as with the siege of a walled town, and the crudely carved gravestones above them carried scenes of hunting or war chariots. Where the palace walls carry fresco paintings the earliest are wholly in the Cretan style, with processional figures, but later there are more lively scenes of chariots or the boar hunt.

In vase decoration the progressive degeneration of the old naturalistic motifs, which had already begun before Knossos fell, continued. Flowers were reduced to patterns of arcs and dots, and eventually the very simplest linear patterns were found to be enough. Some of the larger vases, however, did attract human figure decoration such as was almost completely lacking in Crete. And the scenes, as we might expect, are often of the hunt or chariots, while the monsters, animals and men are strangely stylized into almost vegetable forms [24].

In the engraving of seals the vivid Cretan scenes of animals were replaced by more sober Mycenaean versions of the same subjects, and there is much the same formality and stylization of the figures that is seen on the vases. The ivory-workers turn out rather dull and repetitive plaques for inlaying in furniture and there is hardly one to which we can point as an original artistic creation after the Minoan artists had lost their patrons in their own island, and had trained and been replaced by Greeks in the Greek palaces. The group of two women and

a child from Mycenae [25] was made in the years when Cretan artists must still have been active in Greece.

The tectonic narrative style of Mycenaean art can be discerned in the objects we have discussed. Beside it there is another thoroughly non-Minoan factor, a true feeling for the monumental. We have seen something of it already in the big vases of the Palace Style. In Greece it led to tentative essays in monumental sculpture, like the clay figures of Keos. The obvious example is the Lion Gate at Mycenae, with the two monsters posed heraldically in high relief over the main entry to the citadel [26]. As animal sculpture they must be considered rather poor. In fact, in their conventions and proportions, they are hardly more than Mycenaean seal engraving or ivories monstrously enlarged. It was probably this inability to find an adequate idiom or technique which inhibited further attempts at major sculpture in stone. The Mycenaeans were still too closely bound to the Minoan tradition, in which there was

25. Two women and a child. About 1400 B.C. (Ivory)

26. The Lion Gate at Mycenae. About 1250 B.C.

little which could nourish their feeling for the monumental. In architecture, they did better. The great fortifications of the citadels at Mycenae and Tiryns taught them how to handle great masses of stone fearlessly. The massive beehive tombs which were built for the royal families are miracles of organization and masonry, although more grandiose than cunning as feats of engineering. The royal tomb at Mycenae known as the Treasury of Atreus [27], whose beehive-shaped roof towers to forty-four feet above the floor, gives a good impression of finely jointed masonry and sheer size.

The walls stood to protect the palaces, the tombs were built for the kings, the gold and precious stones were worked for royal patrons. In the twelfth century bands of other Greeks, from the north, swept through the country, overthrew and burnt the palaces. With the palaces, at a single stroke, disappeared the arts which had served them and which they fostered, and the arts of the Minoans and Mycenaeans came to a dead stop. Greece was still occupied by Greeks, but outside the palaces so slight was the artistic life of the country, that there was little if anything to survive at that lower level. And yet, as we shall see, it may be possible to discern something of the character of Mycenaean Greek art in the later and greater centuries of Greek civilization.

27. The tomb 'Treasury of Atreus', Mycenae. 1300–1250 B.C.

2

The Dark Ages: Geometric Greece

There is little enough that either the archaeologist or the historian can do to throw light on the century or more that followed the collapse of the Minoan-Mycenaean civilization. The disappearance of the palace bureaucracies meant the disappearance of the arts they sustained, and even of literacy. The invasions that ravaged Greece, and most of the other countries of the Near East, left behind only primitive village communities in their place. The land was depopulated, and the invaders, themselves Greeks (Dorians), had neither shared in the brilliance of Greece's Mycenaean past nor yet produced anything significant and new of their own to replace it. To Homer and later Greek poets the preceding era was to be the Golden Age of heroes; to the archaeologist, the Bronze Age. But both agree in calling its successor the age of Iron, the metal of the plough and of the sword. In the words of Hesiod:

> For now truly is a race of iron and men will never rest from labour and sorrow by day, from perishing by night; and the gods shall lay sore trouble upon them.

Pottery, always an important source of evidence because of its ubiquity and ready preservation, is now virtually our only evidence of style or civilization. On the vases, themselves degenerate versions of the Mycenaean shapes, we find at the beginning of the Dark Ages the old Bronze Age patterns still in use, their significance lost, and their forms distorted into flaccid and meaningless loops and triangles.

For a picture of society and life in Greece from now down to the eighth century B.C., we have nothing like the cities, cemeteries and palaces which have served us before. We must judge them on the one hand from their art, on the other from the Homeric poems, versions of which must have been sung in these years, and in which something of the society of the times may be detected, overlaid by a veneer of names and stories from the Golden Age. Even the art of writing was forgotten for over 400 years, and where the Minoans and

Mycenaeans left us records of their business affairs (albeit barely intelligible), here there is nothing. Local kings, often hardly more than village chiefs, held their subjects in uneasy allegiance, dependent in part on force of arms, in part on the divine protection of the town's gods. This already presents us with a most significant change. Hitherto the most notable objects had been made for the king and his court: now the best was reserved for the gods. We have left the age of palaces for that of temples, and, since deities are less demanding than mortals, this may be one of the reasons why the craftsmen's products seem to be better distributed throughout the community. But it takes many years before the effect of this is seen. The twelfth and eleventh centuries are the darkest, yet even then, it seems, Greeks were crossing the Aegean to seek fresh land and a securer life on the coastal strip of Asia Minor and its off-shore islands. As the conditions of life gradually became more settled the time was ripe for a reawakening of interest in less material matters.

The crucial moment came in about 1050 B.C., apparently in Athens. We detect it in our inevitable yardstick, painted pottery, and in the sudden contrast between the new vases and the shoddy wares they began to replace. Naturally we cannot say whether this was simply the result of one man's vision. Far more probably it was a fair reflection of the spirit of the age, and may even have had something to do with the invaders or immigrant artists. But it is not the content of Greek art which has changed, simply its treatment. In some strange way Greek artists found it easier to work upon the raw material of Minoan art in its debased, 'sub-Mycenaean' form, than they had done half a millennium before, faced by Minoan art in its prime.

The new 'Protogeometric' pottery of Athens, takes over many of the old shapes and patterns, and presents them in a new way. Technically the pottery is immensely improved. Taut shapes and neat proportions are carefully observed, and the fine black gloss paint matches again the best work of the Bronze Age potters. For the decoration we have still the loops and arcs and triangles of the earlier vases, but where there had been a loose spiral hand-drawn, we now find compass and multiple brush combined to give precise and measured patterns [28].* The disposition of the decoration is also thought

*Horizontal lines were drawn by holding a brush against the pot while it was turned on the wheel: circles were drawn by attaching a multiple brush to a pair of compasses.

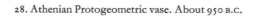
28. Athenian Protogeometric vase. About 950 B.C.

out afresh. It is concentrated at significant points on the vase, which is deliberately articulated into horizontal registers. The main zones of decoration fall at the shoulder or belly, according to where the handles are attached, but the greater part of the vase is left plain, in the colour of the clay ground, with broadly placed stripes. The actual elements of the decoration are indeed fewer than they had been hitherto. The one horse which an artist drew shyly near the handle of an Athenian Protogeometric vase is the exception which points the rule – that figure or floral decoration was excluded.

The over-all effect is as though a completely new discipline had been imposed. A new attitude of mind had enabled the artist to make out of the decadent art of a lost civilization the beginnings of the art of a new one. The new Greek art rose like a phoenix from the ashes of its predecessors.

But, for all the sudden emergence of the Protogeometric style in Athens, its development was extremely slow, and for more than one hundred years its basic principles remained unaltered. They seem to have satisfied both Athenians, and, in time, most of the rest of the Greek world.

At about 900 B.C. the next stage begins – that of the full Geometric style. Athens is again the centre, but this is not a moment marked by any political or social upheaval so far as can be deduced from the archaeological evidence. The population and wealth of the Greek cities were growing steadily and the austerities of the Protogeometric style were beginning to pall. The artist sought to relieve them by experiment with new shapes and new patterns, but these did not wholly replace the old. Certainly he lost interest in the old compass-drawn circles, but many of the new Geometric motifs are developed from the Protogeometric zigzags and triangles. Others, like the meander and swastika, are introduced into the horizontal zones encircling the vase. More of the surface of the vase is covered with such patterns now, and they serve to accentuate this layering of the decoration [29]. The main patterns are saved for the neck, shoulder or belly of the vase, as before, but the rest too may be filled with simpler bands of zigzags or hatched triangles. The whole is finely articulated by the triple lines which divide one zone from the next. On the best vases this regimentation achieves a rhythm which emphasizes the shape, and the earlier Geometric vases on which the bands of pattern are allowed to encircle the vase without interruption seem to show the artist aware of the way it has been built up on the wheel and ready to acknowledge this construction in his painting.

In the eighth century the painter looked for new ways of deploying his geometric patterns, and he began to break up the broad encircling bands into panels of varying widths, and so was able to introduce a secondary, vertical element into the design. A different rhythm is thus established. Square panels filled with, say, swastikas or diamond motifs, might be repeated along the frieze and divided from each other by three vertical strips of zigzags or cross-hatching, each again set off by the usual triple lines. So many of these patterns seem immediately inspired by basketwork that it seems likely that there was influence here from a craft whose products have, of course, not survived. The patterns no longer lead the eye around the vase, but draw attention to particular areas. It was inevitable that larger panels, set prominently on the neck or between the handles of a vase, should attract more intricate geometric patterns, and that these were to offer the fields upon which the artist practised figure decoration for the first time. It is not surprising to find that some scholars have drawn comparisons between this new style of rhythmic decoration and the Homeric hexameter, for this too is the century in which the *Iliad* must have reached its final form, and been written down.

The first figure decoration to appear on Athenian Geometric vases is of horses. We can be sure that possession of a horse was a mark of some importance and wealth, what would now be called a status symbol, and that the representation of the creature might also lend distinction to a work of art. It is followed on the vases by other animals, especially goats and fowl [29]. The Geometric artist approached these subjects in a wholly distinctive way. Individually, the creatures are seen as a sum of their parts, each of which is geometricized – legs into sticks, bodies into long triangles – with emphasis on the most striking features, like the horse's strong neck and mane, or the goat's horns. They are drawn in simple silhouette, with, at first, no inner details admitted whatsoever, not even an eye. When the animals are grouped together the same pose is repeated, whether it be kneeling, walking or grazing, so that the sum of bodies and limbs makes a repetitive geometric pattern of exactly the type that the artist had constructed from his meanders and zigzags. From the outset the animal world

30. Athenian Geometric vase detail: funeral bier and mourners. About 750 B.C.

was subjected to the same geometric discipline as the rest of the artist's stock of motifs.

Human figures are treated in the same way [30]. Now it is the shoulders and legs that are stressed, the torso shown as if in front view as an inverted triangle, and the thighs and calves given strong curves. The figures stand in naked silhouette with plain blob heads. In time some detailing is allowed. The eye is shown by a reserved circle on the head, which grows a chin or beard, and a nose. A small plume suggests the helmet crest of warriors. Strands of long hair appear, and women are differentiated by wearing skirts or, occasionally, by short lines at either side (or sometimes both on one side) of their triangle torsos, to show the breasts. Hands eventually win their full complement of fingers.

Inanimate objects, like furniture or chariots, are treated in a similar manner. Profile and frontal views are combined so that whatever lies beyond an object is often drawn beside it. Chariots show both their wheels and the four-horse teams drawing them usually have all their sixteen legs, four heads and tails clearly visible, and only economize in the bodies. Where a more complicated action is shown, like the raising of a shroud over the body of the dead man [30], its pattern is cut away just above the body so that nothing is obscured by it. This is a very clear example of the artist painting what he knows rather than what he sees – a common enough phenomenon in the history of art, but here also subordinated to broader considerations of design and pattern. The whole scenes, whatever the subject, are composed as geometric patterns, and at a distance the main panel of a large vase presents an orderly pattern of horizontals and verticals which is resolved into details of limbs, bodies, biers or ships only on close inspection.

A good example of the Geometric artist's approach to these figure subjects is given by his treatment of a new animal – a lion. The introduction of this creature, foreign to Greece, was due to a new source of inspiration which will be discussed in greater detail in the next chapter, but the lion, as forerunner of other Eastern monsters, was tamed by the Geometric artist as soon as he appeared. His powerful jaws, teeth, shoulders and claws were the most important features. These were stressed, and the rest of the body was treated as of any other more familiar beast [31]. The Geometric artist and poet shared the same view of the lion – a beast they had probably never seen:

... as easily as does a lion break into the lair of a nimble doe and crush her unweaned fawns, to seize them in his powerful jaws and rob them of their tender life. Even if the doe is close at hand, she cannot help them. She is terrified herself and flies off, crashing through the thicket and sweating in her haste to save herself from the claws of the mighty beast.

Thus was Homer's Agamemnon on the Plain of Troy, and the artist understood the simile.

The most important Geometric figure scenes appear on vases which command our attention for other reasons also. They are the great funeral vases which stood as grave-markers in the cemetery of Athens. It is a reflection of the general growth in prosperity and in personal pride that it should be thought necessary to mark a grave in such a manner. And it is significant that a clay vase should have been chosen. There are various indications which suggest that in the Geometric period the potter and vase painter were among the senior of the artists. This was not by any means an age of extreme affluence, and the potter's materials were, of course, the simplest. So it was perhaps natural that Geometric art found its fullest expression in a craft which demanded extreme technical skill and artistic judgement, rather than material outlay.

The scenes on the large grave vases show various stages in the funeral rites – the laying out of the body with massed mourners [30], and its carriage to the grave. Others show battles on or beside ships. The smaller vases carry a variety of rather simpler scenes. The choice of subject for these first steps in a form of narrative art should be revealing. It is perhaps too much to say, with some, that there seems to be an obsession with death and violence. So many of the finest vases were made specifically for graves, that funeral scenes must be expected, and a scene of violent action is the sort of subject which an artist might well be moved to attempt with his newly won command of figure drawing. The other violent scenes, of lions attacking men or other animals, are inspired by foreign models although treated in the Geometric manner. Of more interest to us are the occasional scenes of dancing, or of sport – duels and boxing – which suggests that although the painter may have been largely bound in his choice of subject by the purpose of his vase and the new eastern fashions which his contemporaries were admiring, yet he still felt free to use more everyday subjects which had no particular symbolic or religious significance – except to the extent that, for a Greek, both play and sport were activities dedicated to the gods.

A more important class of subject is that which includes recognizable mythological scenes. Some may be Homeric, but most represent other stories which were long to be popular in Greek art and literature, especially those featuring the national hero, Herakles (the Roman Hercules). Instead of generalized scenes of action or battle we have specific acts, as of a hero fighting a monster, to which we can put names. When, in a shipwreck scene [32], a mariner is seen to have climbed on to the keel of his upturned ship, we think of Odysseus' shipwreck. The picture could not be more simple or direct. The figures observe the Geometric canon, they thrust at each other with swords, gesticulate, and collapse when stricken, like puppets. They are humourless, without emotion, but they have stopped being patterns and begin to tell a story.

These scenes belong to a period in which the Greeks' horizon was widening as they came to know more of other lands beyond the Aegean, and to a period which saw the crystallizing of the heroic poems into their epic form. 'Homer and Hesiod first gave the Greeks their family of gods' was the way a later writer saw it. By 'codifying' the exploits of the gods and the semi-historical adventures of hero-kings, and especially by committing them to writing, a corpus of myth was established which could fire and feed the imagination of the artist without seriously affecting religious practice or belief. There will be more to say of this connexion between art, myth and religion in a later chapter.

This is the point at which to reflect on the character of this Geometric art, for it represents the last stage of what the post-Mycenaean Greeks worked out for themselves, before the full impact of fresh inspiration from overseas. In it we might hope to distinguish traits which will remain characteristically Greek even when the content and style of Greek art have changed profoundly. And we might hope too to catch an echo of the earlier achievements of Greeks, in the Bronze Age. One of the things which stands out is a true feeling for monumentality, expressed (by necessity) in a medium which is hardly the most suitable – painted pottery. Then there is an overriding sense of pattern, of architectural patterns of friezes and panels which both dominate and express the shapes that carry them – a sense of pattern which is imposed even when human figures are admitted to the decoration; and, finally, once figure scenes appear, a lively interest in narrative, however simple. It will be recalled that these three features – monumentality, a tectonic sense of composition, and interest in narrative – seemed to distinguish Greek Mycenaean art from its Minoan antecedents. We must see how far the same features can be discerned in later centuries, but first there are other aspects of Geometric art to explore, for it was not expressed only on painted vases.

With the growth of prosperity in the eighth century came the demand for more elaborate decoration of everyday objects. Offerings in tombs are generally of things which had been used in life: vases, jewellery, dress pins and the like, but there is another special class of object upon which the artists lavished their best skill, and which include much that is to be considered in this book and its successor – votive offerings. Just as the development of Greek architecture can be told in terms of temple building, for there were no other large important structures in any Greek city (no palaces, for instance), so the dedications to the gods represented the finest products of Greek art. At the great sanctuary of Zeus at Olympia the famous Games were inaugurated in 776 B.C. From about this date onwards the offerings of victors and competitors begin to accumulate, and they give a good idea of the sort of offerings being made in the many humbler sanctuaries of Greece. Some

of these *ex voto*'s may have been everyday objects, given for their intrinsic or decorative value; but many were made specifically for dedication. In the Geometric period they are rarely very elaborate. The commonest are figurines in clay or bronze, often of animals, sometimes of human figures which we are to take as either representations of the deity or substitute attendants to serve him. They are inevitably small – rarely as much as a foot high, most of them under six inches. The technique of handling the clay, and the clay or wax from which the bronze worker made his mould, allowed greater freedom of expression than the geometry imposed by the traditions of vase decoration. Nevertheless, in the great range and variety of Geometric figurines which have been found, we recognize much the same conventions as were observed by the painters. This homogeneity of Greek art at any one time is an important feature, and although in the Geometric and Archaic periods there are strong and distinctive local schools in all the arts, their interrelationship is never particularly hard to discern. Thus, many of the bronze figurines, like the little bronze from Olympia [33], have the stick arms, broad shoulders, nipped waists and bulging thighs of the painted figures. Features are at first not defined in the lump of the head, but in time they take on the angular jutting profiles seen on the latest of the painted vases. A painted clay example is shown here [34]. The free,

34. Head of a man. About 700 B.C. (Clay)

plastic technique also allows some more elaborate poses, but the conventions remain the same. We find a squatting helmet-maker [35] or a lion-hunt group, executed with a brilliant and unlooked-for feeling for composition in the round combined with the sense of balance and proportion which other Geometric Greek art leads us to expect. Other groups are composed of the more stereotyped figures – chariots, a man fighting a centaur [36], animals and their young. As on the vases, horses are popular subjects, and they especially are schematized in bronze in very much the same way as they are by the painters [37]. Both horses and men feature as subsidiary decorations on the bronze tripod cauldrons which are among the grander votives of this period, especially at Olympia where they were probably also prizes for success in the Games.

In the Dark Ages and Protogeometric Athens precious metals were virtually unknown. But in the eighth century gold came into use again, and of the gold work decorated in the Geometric manner there is an important series of bands impressed with animal and human figure scenes. The latter at least closely match those on vases, and the same conventions are observed. The bands themselves were put on the dead, set around their heads, often in such a way as to ensure that the mouth was kept closed. Elaborate *fibulae*, or safety-pins, are usually of bronze, but there are also a few of gold. Where

35. Helmet-maker. About 700 B.C. (Bronze)

36. Hero fighting a centaur. About 750 B.C. (Bronze)

37. Horse. About 750 B.C. (Bronze)

38. *Fibula* safety-pin: stag. About 700 B.C. (Gold)

they have large flat catch-plates or hooks these may be decorated with incision (a stag on [38]), usually in the advanced Geometric manner which admits a great deal more in the way of detail and elaboration.

Finally, of the new arts which eighth-century Greece was learning, or re-learning, comes seal-engraving; at first rather crude square seals of limestone which were probably fitted with wooden handles and used rather like rubber stamps, to impress clay or wax, then other shapes. Where these have figure decoration we see, as on the gold bands, the familiar figure conventions [39].

Once the Bronze Age palaces had fallen their palatial arts disappeared. The patronage on which specialist artists like seal-engravers and fresco-painters had depended was removed, and we may imagine that the artists of the succeeding generations, including those who evolved the Protogeometric style in Athens, were much closer to the artist-craftsman of earlier times in their relationship to the community, and not governed by the demands of a rich upper class. They were the '*demioergoi*' of Homer, almost literally civil servants,

a prophet, a physician, a shipwright, or even a minstrel whose songs might give pleasure. All over the world such guests as these are welcomed.

But some of them were travelling craftsmen whose special skills sought a wider custom than that of their home towns. Even in the Geometric period there is still little sign that the

39. Impression of a seal: bowman and centaur. About 700 B.C.

artists had any other incentive for their work than the simple
need to earn a living, and to satisfy the demands of their
fellows. But these demands were changing rapidly. The gold,
the seals, the elaborate funeral arrangements and ambitious
potting: these all reflect the growing wealth of Geometric
Greece, and were produced to meet a specific new demand.
All this is plain enough when the products of, say, the first
half of the eighth century are compared with those of the
preceding four centuries. The care which the Geometric artist
was prepared to lavish on his work, the strict discipline of his
patterns and the taut geometry of the forms he used betoken a
new self assurance. As this leads to fresh experiments, lively
figure scenes and the representation of men, we are reminded
of that other aspect of the Greek awakening – epic poetry and
Homer. These are still the years of kings and princelings,
cities or states independently building their new prosperity.
Hand in hand with this goes an interest which ranges wider
than local boundaries or walls, the curiosity about peoples
beyond the seas who might provide or teach, who might help
satisfy even a Greek's curiosity. Already in the Geometric age
and in its art we have seen some of the superficial results of this
– the new monsters, the techniques and forms of gold-work
and seal-cutting. So far they have had no effect on the artist's
style, but we are entering upon a new chapter in the history of
western art, in which the newly won confidence of the artists
who evolved the Geometric style in Greece was fired by the
example of foreign works.

3

The Orientalizing Period

If the Protogeometric period saw Greek art in its cradle, and the Geometric its childhood, then the Orientalizing period, of the later eighth and seventh centuries, suffered its adolescence: impressionable years in which the many and varied influences to which it was exposed worked something of a revolution in its outlook, and delinquency was only avoided by the quality and discipline of its early upbringing.

The main source of the new influences lay in the countries of the Near East, but before we study their character and effect the physical and political background to the period may be briefly considered. It should be remarked, however, that in some respects the east had, albeit indirectly, a real effect on Greek society which went beyond the superficial appearance of its arts, and that the course of Greek literature, and of religion and scientific thought, was to be no less profoundly modified. Hesiod's account of the origins of the gods and the dark stories of divine parricide seem to owe much to the stock of Hittite myths which the Greeks would have learnt in Cilicia, but they never claimed so important a position in Greek belief and cult. Some new deities appear (or new forms for old deities) like Cybele, just as later the Greeks were to accept an Egyptian Isis and a Persian Mithras. Lydian and Phrygian modes in music were learnt, and imports ranged from new metal-working techniques, to the domestic hen.

In Greece the small kingdoms were dissolving, and the royal families ousted from their position of power by either the richer landowning families or the representatives of other classes. These might be the fighting men, for warfare was becoming more of a professional matter for the citizen body and less a matter of duels between leaders with mob mêlées; or, more probably, they were the farming or merchant classes. The growth of population and prosperity led to a demand which the resources of Greece itself could not easily meet. There was the demand for raw materials, notably metals, which led to extensive trade in the Mediterranean, and to the foundation of trading posts. And there was the demand for land, which led to the planting of colonies in Italy, Sicily, on the northern shores of the Aegean and even on the Black Sea. These two solutions for the expanding society ran closely together, for the merchants led the colonists, and the colonists could foster and protect trade. Thus it is that the earliest Greek colonies in the west, on Ischia and at Cumae, were founded by the islanders of Euboea at places well set for trade with metal-bearing Etruria, but which were too large or exposed to be regarded as fortresses in a foreign and perhaps hostile land, and which left far behind and nearer home far more favourable farm land. It was these same islanders who, even earlier, had sought out the eastern market. By about 800 B.C. they had reached north Syria and the mouth of the River Orontes, which was throughout history the outlet into the Mediterranean world for the riches of the east. There, at a site now known as Al Mina, they were allowed to set up a trading post, which in time turned into a mainly Greek town. From it the islanders brought to Greece the materials and arts of the east, and in the seventh century they were followed in this by the merchants of east Greece and Aegina.

The effect on Greek artists of this influx of eastern objects and ideas has been the subject of scholarly study for many years. It has never been difficult to list the many motifs which the Greeks borrowed, and with which they broke free from at least some of their Geometric conventions. It is less easy to decide how these motifs were transferred and the extent to which their transference was a matter of mere copying. There can be no doubt that the change which Greek art underwent in these years is almost wholly attributable to the influence of the east, but it is just as clear that this influence was very largely superficial, that the Greeks as pupils were highly selective of what they had to learn, and that they were quick to reject anything which they could not readily assimilate or mould to their own ideas. For this was no matter of an immature art being overwhelmed by the sophistication of the east, but of an already strong artistic tradition deriving new life and inspiration from the forms and subjects of arts which were already in their decline.

This said we can more safely go on to consider what these new influences amounted to. Their effect is seen, on the one hand, in the form of figure drawing and modelling, and, on the other, in the subject matter of the figure and subsidiary decoration. The east had been accustomed to semi-realistic representations of animals and human beings, showing them in simple profile views, with some distortion of limbs or muscles to lend effect, but hardly any realistic detailing of anatomy or drapery, nor any real foreshortening. Still, this was all profoundly different from the Greek Geometric artist's conventions which positively defied nature. From now on limbs and bodies fill out. The Geometric proportions are remembered in the lithe, thin-waisted men and the angular, alert features which offer such a marked contrast with their rather more fleshy and rotund eastern counterparts. But even in accepting this new way of treating figures the Greek artists completely transformed it, for the most explicit examples of the new Orientalizing style are on painted pottery – a medium which was virtually never used for such decoration in the east, certainly in this period. The Greek vase painter observed the eastern bronzes, reliefs and figures in the round, and translated them into silhouette and line drawings. But he did not merely copy them, and the transition from the wholly Geometric pattern-figure to the sinewy Orientalizing one is gradual.

The new subject matter which the East introduced to Greek art was animal and vegetable. The entry of the lion has already been mentioned [31]. Later come monsters which had been known to Bronze Age Greek artists but had now to be tamed afresh. Sphinxes and griffins were the most common, and there was a particular interest in winged monsters, which gives rise to sirens and winged horses – to pull divine chariots or, one of them (Pegasus), to serve in myth. The Greeks added their own monsters, especially the centaur who is met already by the end of the eighth century [36 and 39].

All these new monsters, borrowed or invented, are wholly decorative and only rarely accommodated in myth. The Greeks had their bugaboos and hobgoblins like anyone else but generally did not admit them to their art as the easterners did continually. The monsters we do see are friendly and elegant, never grotesque, sometimes startlingly plausible, like the centaur. The dire eastern griffin could be admitted to a shield blazon, but was shown as a nursing mother! The petrifying gorgon had a grinning lion mask, but by the Classical period could be a beautiful girl with serpentine locks.

Of other creatures the familiar horses, stags, goats and fowl were always to be seen, but cocks and hens appeared on Greek vases only when they first arrived physically in Greece, from the east. Pairs of such creatures grouped heraldically, or processions of them, became the prime feature of many Orientalizing vases [40], and only gave pride of place to scenes with human, heroic or divine figures. It was not until well into the sixth century that the Greek artist was able to rid himself finally of this Orientalizing obsession with animals.

For the subsidiary decoration Geometric bands and patterns gradually died away, and were replaced either by quite simple stripes and rays, or by another eastern contribution – floral patterns. Near Eastern art did not indulge much in the way of landscape, and trees and bushes were reduced to conventional designs. From Egypt were taken over the formal friezes of lotus, bud and palms, and the sacred palm or Tree of Life

40. Protocorinthian alabastron: two stags. About 640 B.C.

appeared in a number of highly stylized forms combining fan-like palmettes and volute scroll branches. These motifs were copied and adapted by the Greeks. In the figured scenes the backgrounds are filled now with floral rosettes or plant-like devices beside or instead of the old Geometric zigzags, for the Greek artist was still preoccupied by *horror vacui*. Lotus and palmette chains ran where before there were meanders or panels. And original, sometimes bizarre, variations on the Tree of Life appear both as centre-pieces for animal groups and as independent compositions. These give a good idea of the way the Greek artist treated these new motifs, for one version, all swirls and volutes, was uprooted by the vase-painters of Corinth [41], twisted into fantastic but neatly balanced patterns, and then abandoned as unsuitable. The other patterns

41. Protocorinthian clay box, base. About 700 B.C.

too were quickly adapted. The outline drawing and stippling which characterized figure drawing was employed to produce cactus-like plant life as in [49]. The lotus and bud or palmette friezes are woven into intricate patterns and in time their form too is changed completely from their eastern models. The lotus, for instance, alternates with the palmette and even begins to grow a palmette from its heart.

These are the outward signs of the Orientalizing movement, inspired simply by looking at objects brought from the east: but there was more direct contact too. In days when artists were not wholly involved in working for palace societies they travelled readily, carrying their tools, and they worked wherever they could. It seems certain that some of the crafts which the Greeks now practised could only have been taught them by personal contact, and could never have been picked up simply by imitation of finished works. This is especially true of ivory-carving and of metalwork. That bronze-workers came into the Greek world from the east seems proved by the startling new works in hammered bronze, both vessels and decorative attachments. In Crete, eastern craftsmen set up a workshop to make votive offerings for local shrines – especially shields for the cave of Zeus on Mount Ida – which are eastern in their form and technique, and at first are eastern too in their decoration, but which gradually admitted more and more Greek motifs and compositions. The Cretan workshop flourished for nearly a century and is wholly distinctive, but there must have been other places, Argos and Samos for example, where Greek artists learned from easterners the techniques for making the great griffin *protomes* which they fixed to cauldrons – at first hammered in the old style, then cast [42]. The griffin, again, is an eastern monster, but the Greek artist tamed it and gave it a decorative elegance which it never had in the east. He picked upon those features which lent themselves best to this purpose – to make a curving, horn-shaped handle. The neck becomes sinuous and serpentine, the gaping bird's beak is menacing and the curve of the upper jaw repeated in the beetling brow over the bulging eyes. Added height is given by the horse ears and forehead knob. In the east it was the whole creature which was generally shown. In Greece its head alone was copied, adapted and translated into a new decorative form.

In ivory the earliest figures carved by a Greek hand are a group of girls (one is illustrated here [43]) found in an

42. Griffin's head. About 650 B.C. (Bronze)

43. Figure of a girl. About 750 B.C. (Ivory)

Athenian grave beside Geometric pottery. Their slim bodies, angular features and the meander on their flat caps proclaim their Greekness, but their pose and caps are derived directly from the ivory figures of the naked goddess Astarte which are so common in the Near East. The eastern figures are plump and rather gross to our eye, parading their sexual and maternal prowess. The Greek artist, once he had learned the technique of carving ivory and acquired the new material, translated his models by paring them of surplus flesh, and giving them the alert geometricized bodies which were more in keeping with the spirit of Greek art in the eighth century. The Love Goddess becomes the 'girl next door'.

Such were the means by which the arts and techniques of the Near East were introduced to the Greek world. Once the models were adopted and the new crafts learnt, the development of Greek Orientalizing art proceeded independently of anything that happened in the Near East, although fresh sources of inspiration continued to be tapped from time to time. The artists worked in the now flourishing city states, and along with the increased prosperity and more ambitious journeys overseas the Greeks became more and more aware of what distinguished them from the barbarian. Their writers were to express this for the realms of politics and thought, notably the Ionian philosophers and, after Greeks had confronted easterners on the field of battle, historians like Herodotus. But in their art too we can perceive the same distinctive quality, even when so much of its content was derived ultimately from the barbarians. Even so, the Orientalizing styles were developed in different ways in different parts of Greece. This is hardly surprising, for this is a lively, formative period, and not until the sixth century do we begin to see again any sort of real unity in the arts all over the Greek world. Intercommunication, even within such a small country, was never very easy. The differences in the regional Orientalizing styles are generally no more than a matter of emphasis. The content is the same but the treatment is in part dictated by one or other of the predominantly Greek attitudes to art which we have already tried to isolate. To a slight extent also differences of race, or even of dialect within Greece itself, and of geography may have contributed to the chequered aspect of Greek art in the later eighth and seventh centuries.

We run the risk of over-simplification if we say that only two main trends can be distinguished, but there is sufficient truth in the generalization and it offers a convenient way of describing the character and course of Greek art in these years.

On the one hand, then, we have the Orientalizing arts of the cities of south Greece, the Peloponnese. These were rich centres, early in touch with the new ideas from the east, quick to adopt new techniques. Their work still carries all the miniaturist precision of Geometric art which is used to deploy the new patterns and forms on pottery, bronzes and small works of clay and stone. On the other hand there is Athens, the islands and, rather belatedly, the eastern Greek cities. These are rather more conservative in their work but they maintain, as the others generally did not, the feeling for monumentality, and it is here that the true beginnings of Greek sculpture are to be sought. This is not a simple racial division – Dorian and Ionian – for Dorian Crete and Rhodes can be classed as readily with their fellow islanders as with their kin in the Peloponnese, and even there Dorian Argos seems to have had much in common with Athens and the islands. Nor is it one of physical opportunity, for the islanders were in fact the first to reach out to the markets of the east. But whatever the cause, and whatever the exceptions, the distinction is a real one, and the art of the islands, Athens and part of central Greece forms a special sort of '*koine*' in the seventh century which had little enough to do with what was happening in the Peloponnese, although at all times there were cross references between the two main groups and sufficient congruity of style for there to be doubts about the provenance rather than the date of many individual works.

Let us look more closely at the works themselves. In the Peloponnese, Corinth led the Greek world in the manufacture of finely decorated pottery from the end of the eighth to the beginning of the sixth centuries. The style in which we see the first Orientalizing features is called Protocorinthian, and the shapes on which they appear are the tiny perfume flasks (*aryballoi*) which travelled far in the Greek world, and some cups and jugs. The Corinthian potters had already begun to shake off the dominance of Athenian Geometric styles in the eighth century, by concentrating on finely executed, extremely delicate and simple linear patterns. One reflection of this is the fondness for broad bands of close-set parallel lines [44] instead of the canonical triple-stripe rhythm of Athenian Geometric. The Corinthians too resisted the Athenian vogue for figure scenes. As a result they were more immediately receptive of

44. Protocorinthian jug. About 730 B.C.

the eastern animal motifs, and, unlike Athens, had no strong
established tradition in figure drawing, which had to be
adapted to the new subjects and ideas. This affected the content of decoration on Corinthian vases throughout this period.
It meant that it reflected more closely the influence and example of the east, and at the same time failed to develop with
any vigour the interest in narrative already apparent in
Athenian Geometric art.

For the animals and animal friezes which were to form an
important element in the decoration of their vases for over a
century the Corinthian painters invented a new technique.
Simple silhouette was not enough, and the occasional detail
reserved in the silhouette could not answer the new interest in
showing muscles and facial features on the more realistic
figures. Moreover the small scale of much of their work pre-
cluded these techniques. Instead, figures were drawn in full
silhouette, and details were then incised upon them with a
point which scratched away the black paint and left the pale

clay showing through [40]. Hitherto decoration on vases had been either painted, or incised, not both, and with the latter the incisions were meant rather to stand out through the shadows caught in them (as in the details on [53]) than to provide linear detail in a contrasting colour. In this respect the new technique was wholly artificial and could only have arisen through imitation of comparable techniques or deliberate invention, and not as a natural development in the existing tradition. The silhouettes are simple brushwork, but the incised details called for the engraver and the draughtsman's skill. Indeed it seems clear that it was the engraved details seen on eastern bronzes and ivories which inspired the use of this technique on Greek pottery. Judicious use of patches of red and white paint was also admitted for highlights, as on ribs, or, more often, to pick out lighter patches of mane or belly. The new incised silhouette technique is called 'black-figure', exactly analogous to the later '*sgraffiato*'.

The hair-line incisions of black-figure encouraged a miniature style, and some of the finest painting on Protocorinthian vases is seen in figures barely one inch high [45]. Rarely, larger figures were drawn (part of a chimaera on [46]), but the

45. Protocorinthian flask (*aryballos*). About 660 B.C.

47. Protocorinthian 'Chigi Vase' detail: horsemen. About 650 B.C.

sparse incised detail is soon lost in the fine sweeping contours of the black silhouette. The older technique of outline drawing was retained for the Orientalizing floral friezes on the vases. Human – or divine – figures appear occasionally amid the rows of animals, and they act out simple mythological scenes. The ever-popular hero Herakles grapples with his various adversaries. Bellerophon rides Pegasus against the monstrous chimaera. Soldiers fight duels, sometimes over the bodies of their dead comrades, and remind us of episodes in the Homeric poems which may also have been in the mind of the artist when he drew them. Rarely the greater part of a vase is devoted to such scenes ([47], from the Chigi Vase). Sometimes inscriptions help us to identify the protagonists. But these narrative scenes are usually subsidiary, and they seldom do more than indicate the Greek interest in this genre which is soon to drive mere animal and floral decoration from the vases.

The popularity of Corinthian vases ensured a vigorous output, but also led to a flood of jejune works which reduplicated the banal animal friezes. Rare experiments with extra colour show the painter attempting something which the scale and setting of his figured friezes could not bear. The Corinthian painter seemed irretrievably committed to his animal frieze decoration – which could only stifle invention. But with it he exercised, perfected and taught a new technique of figure drawing which was to be more subtly and effectively employed by others.

The decorative bronze work produced by Corinth and other cities of the Peloponnese is immediately comparable with the vases. The illustration [48] shows a bronze plaque from Olympia. Two centaurs deal with the invulnerable hero Kaineus in the only way they can – by beating him into the ground with trees. The scene is in essence a symmetrical, heraldic composition of figures and flowers, but it tells a story. The figures are worked in low repoussé and the details are incised. Sometimes incision alone is employed and the lines show dark on the bright, brazen surface (not light on dark as they do on many bronzes today, with talcum-filled lines on a surface darkened by age or treatment). It is important to remember just how much of this early Greek art is essentially that of the draughtsman. This is obvious enough on vases and bronzes, but we shall find it true also of relief sculpture, and, initially, of sculpture in the round.

The influence of the east on Greek sculpture was exerted in a somewhat unusual manner. The Geometric figures of clay and bronze had been freely modelled, and each was an original creation. The east introduced the use of the mould, which was to prove a mixed blessing. Small clay plaques with decoration in high relief, impressed by a mould and showing the naked goddess Astarte, are quite common finds in the Near East. Works of this type reached the Greek world and from them the Greeks learnt the use of the mould, and also copied the figure of the goddess, whom they took for Aphrodite, and soon clothed. Mass production from moulds leads to some

48. Plaque: Kaineus beaten into the ground by centaurs.
About 600 B.C. (Bronze)

degree of standardization in proportions and features. The Greek Orientalizing type for a frontal head in relief copied details of the eastern heads, notably their wig-like hair, but was otherwise more angular, and geometric, with triangular face, large eyes and prominent nose. The bodies of the women are high-waisted and formless, with flat drapery. This is a type which has been called 'Dedalic', after the legendary Cretan artist. It was especially at home in the Peloponnese, but also in Dorian Crete and Rhodes and to some extent all over Greece. It appears on clay plaques, for relief decoration on vases and for figurines, whose bodies are not mould-made but roughly modelled in the hand or thrown on the wheel. The same conventions are applied to other work, like jewellery [59], and to figures in bronze which replace the earlier and more freely modelled Geometric figures. What is more important is that they were also applied to works in stone. Hitherto there had been no stone sculpture in Greece except for isolated pieces in Crete which, on a small scale, closely copied oriental compositions. Now the Dedalic conventions were applied to statuettes and relief figures carved in soft limestone, to serve as votive offerings or as decoration on temples, and these began to achieve some degree of elaboration. Their drapery and features were tricked out in bright colours. The Auxerre goddess in the Louvre [56a], for example, carries traces of the bright paint on her dress. The soft stone could be cut almost as easily as wood, and we can be sure that wood was used also for cult statues. Of this there is evidence in ancient authors, but the only wooden objects which have survived are of a very small size. Occasional wooden figures had been covered with hammered bronze sheets (the '*sphyrelaton*' technique) and these give some idea of the probable appearance of other minor wooden statuary.

The Dedalic conventions for sculpture and the black-figure technique for drawing on vases are the two major components of our first main group of Orientalizing works. They were important stages in the development of Greek art, and yet it must be admitted that, for a while, they suppressed other qualities which we value in the Geometric art which went before. The free modelling of some earlier figurines is sacrificed to the tyranny of the mould and the new conventions which it brought with it. On the other hand the discipline and pattern of Geometric vase painting is gradually lost to less organized animal and vegetable designs, and although black-figure gave opportunities for the exercise of that precision which always characterized the best in Greek art, it could also lead to fussy and repetitive composition. Something of these qualities was saved in the more conservative second group of Orientalizing works, to which we now turn.

In the Geometric period Athens and the islands established a strong tradition in figure drawing on vases. When the new patterns from the east began to become familiar in Greece this tradition, as we have seen, was still strong enough to mould the new forms to the Geometric canon. Later, as the Orientalizing flood grew, the painters made more concessions to it. Plain silhouette gave place to outline drawing. The figures were rendered with greater detail, but their proportions and features remained strongly Geometric; and although this drawing must be taken as symptomatic of the Orientalizing movement, it shows nothing in the way of direct imitation of anything oriental. The subsidiary decoration reflects the new ideas more clearly. The backgrounds were filled with floral rosettes, while dotted cactus-like shrubs start from the ground [49]. Less conspicuous parts of the vases are covered with

49. Proto-attic lid: horses and foal. By the Analatos Painter. About 700 B.C.

50. Proto-attic vase detail: Odysseus blinding Polyphemus. About 650 B.C.

interlace patterns. Many of the motifs own the same inspiration as those seen on Corinth's vases, but they were being used here with an exuberance, sometimes rather slapdash, which produces a quite different effect from that of the precise miniaturist work of Corinthian artists. This is in part simply a matter of scale. The great Athenian funeral vases of the Geometric period lived on in the tall grave amphorae of the seventh century, but instead of the mannered rows of Geometric patterns the whole body of the vase was filled with sweeping figure compositions. Monumentality could still be achieved even when the decoration had become of a type which draws attention to its subject matter rather than to the shape of the vase it covers.

The content of the decoration too was different. Narrative scenes of myth and heroic battles took pride of place. The animals and animal friezes which are found on Corinth's vases were relegated to positions of minor importance, but the individual creatures were executed with a verve and emphasis which still carries much of the Geometric artists' conception of figures as patterns. On a vase found at Eleusis Odysseus leads his comrades in blinding the monstrous Polyphemus (Cyclops), stupefied by wine [50]. In the islands we still see animals [51] beside the curvilinear ornament, and the form of

51. Griffin jug. About 650 B.C.

52. Island vase fragment: Artemis and a lion. About 600 B.C.

the new, hellenized griffin heads, which we have met in
bronze [42], is used for the neck of a jug. There are pleasing
touches of originality and humour too for which we look in
vain among the precise regiments of Corinth's zoo. Grass-
hoppers crawl idly up the picture frame, water birds browse
unconcerned between the legs of battling monsters, imps of
the artist's own creation pirouette together beneath the handles
of a vase. The figures are drawn to a scale commensurate with
the size of the vase, and may be anything up to two feet in
height. That the artist was conscious of more than the simple
effect of outline drawing is shown by the way he comes to
attempt decorative effects by the contrast of areas of white and
black both on figures and on the subsidiary ornaments [50].
This led inevitably to the use of colour and the beginning of a
true polychromy which was never to be wholly successful on
Greek vases. Not only were touches of red and white used for

details, but whole areas of limbs or drapery were covered with a wash of white or brown. This was a technique which the islands, rather than Athens, came to favour, and the vogue for it lingered there long after it had been abandoned in mainland Greece. From one of the islands comes part of a large funeral vase [52] showing the winged goddess Artemis seizing her lion by ear and tail. This is a more advanced example of the outline style, with more colour, but it admits here and there (on wings and the animal) the foreign 'black-figure' incisions which are still used very sparsely on the Athenian vase ([50], on hair and beard).

In those areas of the Greek world in which this style of vase decoration was current – Athens, parts of central Greece and the islands – very similar decoration was applied to other objects. We see the same figures on the large clay vases which are not painted, but decorated with figures in low relief. On one [53] Perseus decapitates the horse-Medusa on a relief vase from central Greece (Boeotia) which belongs to a class that seems to have originated in the islands. There is not so much bronze work as we have from the Peloponnese, but what there is carries incised figures which stand gaunt and angular beside the neat engraving of Corinth or Argos. Some cut-out plaques from Crete offer a more lively style, notably the hunter lifting his quarry, a bound goat [54]. The way the man's head can be

53. Relief vase detail: Perseus decapitates the horse-Medusa. About 630 B.C.

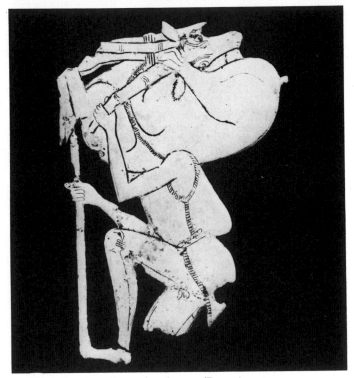

54. Plaque: hunter and goat. 650–625 B.C. (Bronze)

obscured is a feature which was not generally tolerated in
Greek art at this time. The piece is shown here in a negative
photograph which restores something of the effect of the
bright surface and dark incisions of the original.

In eastern Greece – Rhodes and the islands and cities of
Ionia – Orientalizing art comparable with that of the rest of the
Greek world made its appearance more slowly. This may seem
strange, since the East Greeks were among the first to join in
the exploitation of the Near Eastern markets; perhaps conservatism, or lack of contact with homeland Greece, made
them laggard. When Orientalizing decoration does appear on
their vases it is in the silhouette and outline technique of the
islands, but its style is quite different and illustrates yet another
way in which oriental patterns influenced Greek lands. This is
what is known as the Wild Goat Style: animal friezes of goats

55. Rhodian vase. About 600 B.C.

and other animals predominate [55] and figure scenes of
myth are almost unknown. The backgrounds are filled with a
great variety of floral and geometric patterns and give a
tapestry effect which has suggested to some that the style was
directly inspired by eastern embroideries. Be that as it may, the
fact remains that the East Greeks evolved a vase painting
style which, while it exploits all the same Orientalizing patterns as those current in the rest of Greece, remains utterly distinctive. It is a good measure of the independence and variety
of Greek artists' response to the new stimulus.

In the plastic arts the Dedalic style was not unknown to the
islanders and East Greeks, but the freer modelling in clay and
the exaggerated, angular features of earlier days still survived.
Yet it is in this sphere – which we have characterized for its
conservatism and tenacious appreciation of monumental

qualities – that we see the true beginnings of Greek sculpture.

The source of inspiration came, again, from overseas. In the seventh century the eastern Greeks had taken over from the Euboeans the prime interest in the trading post at Al Mina in north Syria. After the middle of the century they initiated a similar enterprise in Egypt, with the foundation of another trading post, conceded by the Egyptian king, at Naucratis in the Nile Delta. The way had been paved by Greek mercenaries employed by the pharaohs. Some of the Greeks stayed behind, and soon a regular township, sponsored by various East Greek states and by the island of Aegina, grew up as the recognized entrepôt for all Greek trade with Egypt.

In Egypt Greeks, and, we may be sure, Greek artists, were faced by an art of a character utterly different from what they found in the Near East. What must have impressed them most is exactly what still impresses latter-day fugitives from Hellenic cruises who are carried up the Nile – monumental stone sculpture and monumental stone architecture.

The sculpture presented two novelties to the Greeks: figures of life size or more, and the use of a hard stone. They were accustomed to statuettes in soft limestone, clay or wood. The physical appearance of the Egyptian statues was less unusual, for the standing figures with one leg advanced and hands to the side were already familiar in their small bronzes, and when they came to make large statues they found no need to copy details of Egyptian stance or dress. And for a hard stone, to match the Egyptian's basalt and granite, they had to look no farther than their own islands where fine white marble could be easily quarried from the surface and worked with emery, and iron tools. After a millennium and a half [2] the islands' resources were to serve artists again. The first attempts at monumental sculpture are found in the islands. The earliest whole surviving piece is a statue of a woman, made for dedication on the sacred island of Delos by a Naxian [56b]. The conventions for the figure and head are Dedalic, for in Greece at this time there were no others to apply for female figures. This has led many to date the figure too early, misled by both its appearance and the awkward, angular cutting of the new material which the artists had yet to master. This lady, the dedication of Nicandre, regularly appears in books on Greek sculpture as typically Dedalic, and is shown beside the Auxerre goddess [56a] in pictures which reduce them disproportionately to appear the same size. The real measure of the difference between them, the difference between the old and the new approach to statuary, can be understood only when it is remembered that one is cut in soft limestone, the other in hard crystalline marble, that one is a statuette, the other over life size. Shown side by side as in the casts illustrated [56] they can be appreciated, one, as the simple embodiment of a rigid decorative convention, the other, as the application of that convention, for want of any other, to a statue conceived with an utterly different purpose and for an utterly different effect.

After Nicandre's statue the interest of sculptors was engaged rather by the challenge offered by representations of the nude male figure, a far more difficult proposition than the columnar, clothed women. Their achievements in this, and the development of the '*kouros*' type will be described in the next chapter, but there are some elements in the early statues which reflect their Egyptian inspiration and deserve to be noted. For there was a real danger that, like the Dedalic, the new marble statuary would be bound by quasi-mathematical conventions. Statues of this type were carved by cutting back from outlines drawn on the sides of the rectangular block of marble. This is why the figures are so four-square, and even near rectangular in section; why their features are pushed to the front plane of the face; why the patterns of ear, eye or knee are applied much as the vase painter applied them, and not organically related to the body. In Egypt the drawings from which the statuary was carved were laid out according to a set canon of proportion for all parts of the body; and there was a danger that this almost mechanical method of composition would be copied by the Greeks. The earliest of the complete marble *kouroi* to survive [57], now in New York, does in fact observe the Egyptian canon, and Diodorus told the story of sixth-century bronze-workers who also followed it. But the canon was soon abandoned, and the other early marble statues are not bound by conventional proportions.

The very earliest of the *kouroi* from the islands – exemplified by the small bronze [58], since no complete marbles survive – retained, like Nicandre's statue, the Dedalic conventions for the head. But we shall see that it is this new tradition of marble statuary, and not the Dedalic, which marks the true beginning of Greek monumental sculpture – in much the same way as the outline-drawn figures on the vases were to have more in common with later achievements in vase decoration than the apparently more go-ahead black-figure of

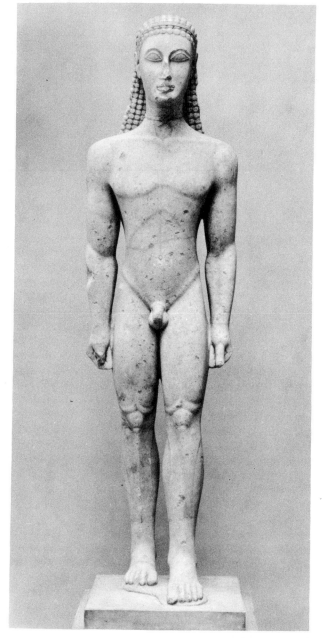

58. *Kouros.* About 620 B.C. (Bronze)

Corinth. In some ways it was in the conservatism, the more essential Greekness, of the arts of Athens and the islands, that their strength lay, but the new styles of the Peloponnesian cities were to play their part too, and it is the confluence of these two traditions that produced the finest examples of mature Archaic art.

The vases, bronzes and sculpture which we have discussed, appear generally either as dedications in sanctuaries, or as offerings in tombs. There is no question of their being reserved for palaces – for there were none – and quite humble cemeteries may yield one or two masterpieces, the possessions of folk who could not afford much in the way of the more elaborate goods, but who would appreciate them and were in no way debarred from buying them when they could. But this was a period of growing prosperity and there must have been many more families able to indulge a taste for luxury objects than hitherto. As a result there was greater activity by the workers of precious metals and ivory, and by seal-engravers, inspired both by eastern models and by the growing demand for their work.

Among the more popular forms of jewellery are gold plaque pendants with figures worked in low relief and details often rendered by granulation [59]. Ear-rings are fastened

59. Plaques: Artemis with lions. About 625 B.C. (Gold)

60. Ear-ring pendant: griffin heads. About 625 B.C.

with long pendants ending in griffin's heads, worked in the round, with details in filigree and granulation [60], and there are floral disks with miniature animals' heads, flies or blossoms worked in the same technique. The human figures and heads are generally Dedalic in their proportions, and much of this work seems to have been done in the Greek islands.

In ivory too we find a number of minor works exquisitely carved, which are either in the Dedalic style or are more closely modelled on Eastern ivories. The kneeling youth from Samos [61] may have decorated a lyre. A particularly important series of ivory objects are the disk seals which were being made in the Peloponnese in the seventh century. These are carved, usually on both faces, with Orientalizing animals and occasionally figure scenes, in shallow intaglio (impression in [62a]). It is, admittedly, doubtful whether they were ever much used as seals, and their prime purpose may have been purely decorative, even as beads and pendants or on wristlets. Their production was inspired largely by the widespread seal usage in Near Eastern lands and their shapes by some of the Geometric stone seals which had been cut in Greece.

61. Kneeling youth. 625–600 B.C. (Ivory)

a

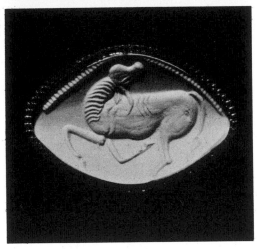

b

The ivory seals are of the Peloponnese, of Corinth, Argos and Sparta. Matching them, but in stone, are seals which were made in the Greek islands, most probably on Melos (an impression in [62b]). These are of an importance and interest far beyond their intrinsic merit, because they show us how artists could be influenced by the arts and artefacts of a past civilization, otherwise remembered only by the poets. Melos had been an important island in the Bronze Age, rich in objects of both Minoan and Mycenaean type, including seal-stones. In the seventh century it seems that seals from Bronze Age tombs were being found in the island, by tomb-robbers or quite accidentally, and that they caught the attention of local artists. This sort of thing can easily happen and in the last century collectors, who sought out these seals, found many fine specimens being worn still by Greek peasants. But the Melians were not content with admiring or wearing the old engraved gems. Their artists copied the two most distinctive shapes – the lentoid and amygdaloid – in a soft local stone, generally pale green in colour. The devices they chose are at first roughly Geometric, cut boldly but with little finesse, the ordinary Orientalizing animals. But on occasion they copied the devices of the Bronze Age seals too, the form of the Minoan griffin, the torsional representation of animals, and other specific motifs and compositions which were foreign to Orientalizing Greek art. These island gems were being made for something like a century or more, and, once again, it is their technique and style rather than the Peloponnesian ivories which are to provide the direct inspiration for later Greek gem engraving.

The island gems provide the most striking instance of a throw-back to Bronze Age forms. The Minoan-Mycenaean world left few monuments of architecture or sculpture above ground to be observed in later centuries. In Archaic Greece, as still today, prehistoric objects must have been found in some quantity on the old palace sites, and certainly there was deliberate tomb-robbing – the richest of the tombs became known as treasuries. The interruption in the practice of the more specialist arts after the Bronze Age was virtually complete in Greece, and only some trivial decorative motifs on coarse pottery and some vase shapes survived in use. So any other reflections of Bronze Age art should probably be attributed to chance finds of the kind described.

We have already remarked that the ultimate purpose of many of the finer objects was to serve as offerings in a shrine or tomb, but it is clear that most of them also served to gladden the eyes of the living. We look in vain at Greek Orientalizing art for anything which we might call religious art. Appropriate figures of a deity were fashioned for dedication in his shrine, but more often than not the votives may represent the worshipper or, when they are not intrinsically valuable objects themselves, are tokens of some richer offering. The mythological scenes on the vases show the gods in action, but the spirit is generally one of naïve story-telling and as far from any real sense of the religious significance of the stories as are the passages in the epic poems which may have inspired the pictures. Consider only Hephaestus' fall from Olympus (p. 135) or Homer's story of how the lame god netted Ares and Aphrodite in bed together.

The Greeks liked telling stories, and their interest in narrative was already coming to the fore in their art. Otherwise its content is determined by the decorative effect of the models which were selected and adopted into the artist's repertoire from overseas. Hand in hand with this interest in showing human beings and heroes in action and in making votive images of and for the anthropomorphic gods, there grew the characteristic Greek interest in representing the human body. This is, of course, better shown in the succeeding periods, and in the seventh century there was strong competition for the artist's attention from animals, and to a lesser extent from floral and abstract patterns. Yet the idea of 'heroic nudity' seems already born. The Geometric figures represent man, *tout simple*, quite untrammelled by dress. In the seventh century the more explicit battle scenes very often show the warriors naked but for their weapons and helmets, and wearing no protection or covering for their chests and loins, such as they must have worn in life. The warrior god Zeus is shown naked, too, but for helmet and belt. Even when bronze armour is worn it is modelled and decorated to represent the forms of the naked body beneath. At Olympia stories were told about the first man who dropped his loin-cloth in the games, ran naked and won. A modern athlete might think lack of support and covering at the loins a positive handicap, but the story may have been a late explanation for a phenomenon which the Greeks had come to realize was not the rule outside their country.

This conscious pride in the human body is already becoming dominant in the Orientalizing period, and the spirit is one reflected in other spheres of Greek life. The proper study of mankind was, for artist and philosopher, man. And not woman, be it noted. Save for a few deliberate imitations of the naked eastern Astarte, female figures are regularly clothed. There was nothing divine about the female form to the seventh-century artist. And it was soon to be suggested that there was precious little of the divine about love for women. This was a prejudice which could be righted only when the life and work of women were more openly acknowledged. But the age of Sappho was not far away.

Finally, there are some qualifications and cautions, those made at the start of this chapter which should be repeated before we leave the Orientalizing period. It is easy to think of Greek art in these years as being no more than a sort of provincial extension of the arts of the Near East. This is manifestly untrue, and it may even be that we over-estimate the effect of the eastern models. The game of what might have been ('had Cleopatra's nose been longer . . .') is one decried by historians but none the less readily played. So, we may ask, what would have been the development of Greek art if Near Eastern art had not been what it was and the Greeks had not shown the interest in it that they did? First, I fancy that the native Greek feeling for pattern, draughtsmanship and monumentality would have had its way in time. Secondly, I have the suspicion that it may have had its way quicker. Consider the two main subjects that we can observe. In vase painting the black-figure technique, a direct outcome of eastern influence, was so restricted and conventional that for more than a century there was virtually no advance in skills in composition of groups or figures. But when it was shaken off and the free-hand drawing of red-figure adopted, the changes came thick and fast, and within a generation artists commanded a line which Michelangelo might have envied, instead of the marionette-like actors of black-figure scenes. In sculpture the east introduced the mould and the Dedalic style. The refined pattern of the latest Geometric art was replaced by a sterile frontal convention which remained virtually unchanged for more than half a century. Only the monumental aspirations of the Greeks and the challenge of harder materials enabled them to rise above it, and even then there must have been some danger of their falling into the even more sterile and conventional manners of

Egyptian sculpture. It is too easy to think of the development of Greek art as a bold imaginative progress, ever forward. There are some aspects of Orientalizing Greek art which might make one think that this was a period of marking time, if not of positive retrogression in some fields.

In a century or so most of the oriental elements were to be worked out of the tradition. We have to dwell upon the sources of eastern influence, acknowledged by Greek artists, if only to see how their native skill completely translated and adapted what they borrowed. They chose carefully, never merely copied, and the motifs or techniques which they learnt they soon turned into something which can be recognized as being more wholly Greek than Orientalizing or Egyptianizing. It is the process by which they assimilated these influences which should be the main subject of any study of Greek Orientalizing art, for in it is revealed those qualities which are essentially Greek, which were apparent already in Geometric Greece, and which make even the most exotic product of Greek craftsmen in these years readily distinguishable from the work of their overseas colleagues and mentors. It was in the seventh century and through Greece that the great civilizations of the Nile and Mesopotamian valleys made their contribution to the history of western art. In later years influence and instruction were to pass in the opposite direction.

4

The Archaic Period
of the Sixth Century

The sixth century B.C. saw the establishment of all the major arts which were to reach full maturity in the following classical period – the definition of the main orders of architecture, and new techniques for sculpture and vase painting. It saw the Orientalizing art of Greece purged of all that seems foreign, so that although the eastern origins of much that remained can still readily be traced, further development is an internal matter, dictated wholly by Greek taste and standards. Moreover, at the end of this period the Greeks had physically to face the direst threats to their independence from the barbarian – the Persians in the east, the Carthaginians in the west. Their successes strengthened their sense of freedom and made them even more fully aware of those characteristics of speech and thought which distinguished them from the barbarians.

It was a period in which the Greek city state changed rapidly in its constitution and character. The old royal houses had lost their power, and control had generally passed into the hands of small groups who owed their position to wealth or influence, or of a single man – a 'tyrant'. These tyrants were not as oppressive or cruel as present-day usage of the word implies. Their courts seem often to have attracted artists, and several tyrants initiated important public works. These courts served as a sort of focus for artistic activity such as had not been provided in Geometric or Orientalizing Greece, except, to some degree, at the great national sanctuaries. Finally, true democratic institutions were already being worked out in some states, in East Greece and in Athens. But it was only later to be shown that state patronage for the arts could be as effective as personal patronage.

Bronze vases were probably by now becoming more common, and were certainly more valuable than the clay ones, but they offered less opportunity for the sort of graphic decoration which we find so informative.

Painted clay vases once again offer us the fullest sequence for a study of the arts in this period. We can follow their development, the work of individual artists and local schools, in considerable detail.

In the seventh century Corinth had perfected her miniaturist black-figure technique for vases, while Athenian artists remained more conservative, with their outline drawing, and could still express the monumental in this difficult medium. By the end of the century Corinth's success in the markets of the Greek world led to much coarse work, and the animal frieze style was already limping badly. Athenian artists, no competitors hitherto, then accepted the black-figure technique wholeheartedly and successfully adapted it to the scale and importance of the vases they were used to decorating [63]. This felicitous union of the two major trends in Orientalizing Greek vase painting led to the most familiar, entertaining and prolific of all the black-figure schools, and it meant that Athens was in time able to drive Corinthian vases from the Greek markets.

The details of this competition can be followed and make an absorbing story. First, Athens' acceptance of the new (to her) technique, her mastery of it and a period of imitation of Corinthian work; then her confidence in it, and Corinth's response with the challenge of colour, leading by the middle of the sixth century to the extinction of the vase painter's art in Corinth's potters' quarter, at least as far as clay vases went. But Athens had to pay a price. Not many of her early black-figure vases admit the grand narrative scenes of myth. Great animals crowd into the panels, and on some vases the animal friezes of Corinth begin to pace as wearily and aimlessly as ever. The best artists could lend spirit as well as precision to their animal studies [64], and even to the smaller creatures in the friezes, but their real contributions still lay in the portrayal of scenes of myth. By the middle of the sixth century the blight of animal friezes had been removed, and the primary decoration of all vases was composed of figure panels or friezes, either large or miniature in scale, with a variety of scenes which will be discussed later in this chapter. The old Orientalizing animals and floral patterns were forgotten, or banished to trivial positions, on lips and rims. The floral friezes were still used to frame pictures though by now in much changed form, and under handles the artist essayed palmette and scroll compositions [as on 68] of an elegance which his Orientalizing,

63. Athenian black-figure vase detail: griffin. By the Nessos Painter. About 620 B.C.

64. Athenian black-figure jug: lion. By the Gorgon Painter.
About 590 B.C.

and indeed oriental, colleagues of earlier years could never have imagined.

The conventions of the Athenian black-figure style did not allow of any great originality of composition. Figures were allowed to overlap, but they had their feet firmly planted on the ground and there is no suggestion of perspective or foreshortening. Runners are shown as if kneeling, with their elbows thrown out, and there was no attempt to show realistically the twist at the junction of the frontal torso and the profile legs. Not until the middle of the century does drapery hang in real folds or follow the lines of the body beneath. There are colour conventions too. In Egyptian painting men are painted red, women white. In black-figure women's flesh is painted white, but the men's left natural – in this case black! Some of the earlier black-figure vases show men and monsters with weather-beaten red faces, and when the men undress we see that they have sun-burnt chests too. This is a reasonable convention in itself, but slightly ridiculous when the rest of the body is black, and it was soon abandoned.

Athens was not the only Greek city to produce black-figure vases, but her potteries were the most prolific and successful. Among the other Greek states and the colonists in the west there were also independent schools [65]. Workshops were set up in Etruria by expatriate artists from East Greece, to which we shall return later. But it was the Athenian style which was dominant, and all the others acknowledged its supremacy by imitation. Inevitably it was in Athens that the next revolution in vase-painting technique was effected.

65. Chalcidian cup: eyes and a maenad. By the Phineus Painter. About 530 B.C.

Black-figure had its limitations. The tenuous scratched lines offered no opportunities for varying stress of detail, and the added colours lent a fussy rather than a true polychrome effect. For over half a century the conventions for drawing features or drapery had remained virtually unaltered, and although Athenian artists were able to achieve works of considerable decorative merit, even works of dignity and of high spirit, still the trammels of their technique seemed likely to stifle their invention as it had the Corinthians. Like the Dedalic style for sculpture, it seemed to lead nowhere. The solution was found (in about 530 B.C.) in a reversion to the old technique of outline drawing by brush, and the abandonment of the engraver. It had never been wholly forgotten by Athenian artists, and several had retained the technique for women's heads and bodies [as in 90]. In a way it was like putting the clock back nearly a century, but it may be just as reasonable to regard Athenian black-figure as an interruption, albeit a distinguished one, in the natural development of the vase painter's craft.

Yet the new outline drawing was not a simple reversion to the old. It was quite literally the negative of black-figure, and around the drawn outlines the background is filled in completely with black so that the figures stand out in the red colour of the clay – whence the name, 'red-figure'. Orientalizing

66. Athenian white-ground cup fragment: Triton. By the Eleusis Painter. About 500 B.C.

Cretan artists had anticipated the new technique on some vases, but do not bring their black right up to the outlines of the figures. There are two possible reasons for the change. Outline-drawn figures without the filled background perhaps looked too inconspicuous, but there are some abortive attempts at red-figure without the black background, and some on a specially prepared white background (like the fragment shown here [66] with the sea monster Triton and a dolphin). The light-on-dark figures might equally, however, have been inspired by the appearance of contemporary relief sculpture, in which the figures were lightly coloured or left in the natural stone against a background painted deep red or blue. Whatever the reason, the new technique gave the artist some measure of the freedom he required, and in time enabled him to suggest figures and objects three-dimensionally in a way denied to the 'black-figure' painter. Free brushwork encouraged subtler detail, thin paint suggested ribs and muscles, a heavier relief line lent a sharp sparkling definition to important lines or contours [67]. Three-quarter views of bodies were

68. Athenian red-figure cup: flute girl with wine jar. About 510 B.C.

successfully attempted, limbs were shown foreshortened, the eye at last in true profile view in a profile head. The drapery takes on a softness of texture, and its folds hang in an exuberance of pleats and zigzag hems. There is a new vitality in both the execution and the subjects, and the value of simple line for detailed anatomical drawing was not forgotten. Black-figure lingered on for a while for trivial vases and for the traditional vases given as prizes in the Panathenaic Games. But the new technique was to be the last word in figure decoration, and when it too was eventually played out, in the fourth century, painted figure decoration for vases also disappeared.

The problems of suiting the decoration of the vase to its shape were not faced as honestly as they had been in, say, Minoan Crete, or in the Protogeometric and Geometric periods. The potter continued to throw elegant shapes of such immaculate proportions that some have thought that they were worked out mathematically. But because perfect proportions can be expressed in numbers, it does not mean that they can be derived only from numbers. There is nothing to suggest that anything like a template was used by the potter in throwing his vases, and the skill of the modern peasant potter in reproducing series of vases of exactly the same size and shape without mechanical aids should warn us against seeing too much science in the ancient potter's art. The open mixing bowls, the neat jugs, and the shallow cups on their high stems all served to grace the table, and there is no suggestion that the shapes were in any way dictated by the elaborate figure decoration that many of them carried. This decoration sometimes fitted well enough, where either side of a straight-sided bowl gave a near rectangular panel. The cups offered inside a *tondo* frame which, on vases, coins and gems, the Greek artist filled successfully either with single running figures, or groups, and in time most subtly with figures and poses which fit with ease this most difficult of fields. Often an artificial ground line is drawn, or the curved border serves, but there are rare examples (generally outside Athens) of whirligigs or similar compositions. The outsides offered two arc friezes. On one example [68] the pattern of eyes is one taken over from black-figure. Between them are the red-figure palmettes, against one of which a naked girl has propped her cushion while she examines the contents of a wine jar and swings her flute-case idly from one foot. Sometimes, however, the figures sit unhappily on the vase; its curves foreshorten them grotesquely, their heads disappear round corners. It is only in the simpler compositions that the two crafts – of potter and painter – seem happily married. Otherwise, it must be confessed that the type of figure drawing which the Greek artists favoured was on the whole unsatisfactory for pottery decoration. In time the artist's work was to suffer too from the inhibiting effect of the uncompromising black background forcing his figures to the front of the stage and denying depth of action. And although to us one of the main attractions of red-figure is its simple black and white effect, the artist was also in time to hanker after more colour. The first generation of red-figure artists, undisturbed by these considerations, offers us the most satisfying examples of the new technique.

The patterns of limbs and muscles, bodies and dress, which we find on sixth-century vases, offer a steady progression towards a more realistic and accurate representation of the human body. In sculpture the story is much the same. The sense of pattern and proportion is unimpaired, but a growing mastery of technique, and more detailed observation of nature, gave the sculptor a greater range of expression. The '*kouros*' figures of naked youths retain the old, hieratic pose unaltered, eyes front, hands lightly clenched at the sides, one leg advanced [69]. In the rendering of their limbs and features, however, they change considerably. Details of eye, ear and hair become more natural [70]; the features relax and soften, and the head may be gently inclined. The charming but tense archaic smile disappears as the earnest and hopeful expressions give way to the idealized and relaxed. A good example of the new treatment of the head can be seen in the recently found clay head of Athena from Olympia [71]. The colour on the fired clay has survived better than the painting has on most marble statuary. The rectangular block from which the marble statues were hewn is gradually forgotten and the bodies are realistically rendered. But they are not yet to be seen from any viewpoint other than the front or sides. This much the old technique and the rigid stance still imposed, and in the sixth century the sculptural advances are on the whole more 'linear' than volumetric.

The earliest of the life-size female figures in marble had been cut according to the old Dedalic conventions and proportions [56b]. She had few followers. One or two early sixth-century figures have the long heavy build and features of the early *kouroi*, especially those from Athens, and their dress hangs in

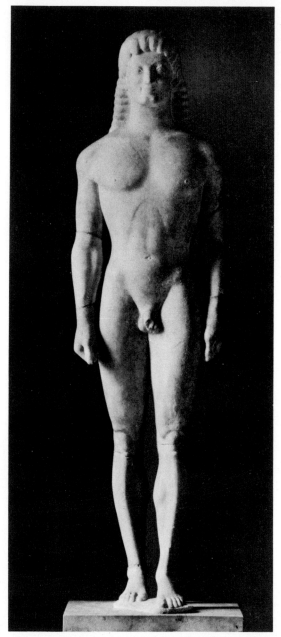

69. *Kouros.* About 550 B.C.

70. (Left) *Kouros* head. About 530 B.C.

71. Head of Athena. About 490 B.C. (Clay)

flat, shapeless folds. Soon, however, the eastern Greeks took a hand in the development of this statuary type. They seem always to have been more attracted to superficial decoration and colourful, even fussy patterns. This appears in their jewellery, vases, even their architecture. It was they who saw the possibilities offered by the texture and hanging folds of a woman's dress, and they exploited this patterning of drapery with scant attention to the form of the body beneath, except in so far as it served as a sort of lay figure [72]. These statues of women (*korai*) adopt as rigid a stance as their brothers. Across the upper part of the body a diagonal feature is provided by the cloak (*himation*) slung around one shoulder. The pattern is answered below by the folds pulled by the hand to one side of the legs – a gesture which at first was shown mainly to diversify the pattern of the folds, but which later served as an excuse to carve in full detail the legs and buttocks, revealed through the thin, taut drapery. The rich dress was heightened by intricate coloured patterns which were added to the marble. We know most about these *korai* not from East Greece itself but from Athens. The Persian sack of the Acropolis in 480 B.C. shattered the statuary upon it, including many votive offerings of *korai* – attendants for the goddess. These were kept by the Athenians when they returned to their city after the battle of Salamis, and buried on the Acropolis. While these figures tell best the story of the Athenian *korai*, the influence of East Greece is unmistakable. Some pieces can be recognized from their style as being from the hands of Ionians [72], and Ionian Greek sculptors signed some of the extant statue bases.

Free-standing groups of statuary were unknown in the Archaic period, apart from assemblages of the stock *kouroi*, *korai* or reclining figures. But if there was little variety in the types of statuary in the round, relief sculpture afforded a field in which the sculptor could exercise his interest both in more varied poses and in narrative, almost as freely as could the vase painter. In fact most Archaic relief sculpture clearly reveals its origin in line drawing on the face of the slab, the background cut away and most detail left in the front plane. In Athens gravestones were carved with a figure (rarely more than one) representing the dead as once alive, although not in action. The warrior or athlete stands with his spear or discus [73]; a woman is shown with her child. The relief is very shallow and the heads are, of course, invariably in the simple profile view, but the sculptor still found it possible to render

73. Gravestone fragment: youth with discus. About 550 B.C.

considerable detail, and the features were carved with the
delicacy and precision which we always associate with the best
Greek Archaic works. The earlier gravestones are topped by
sphinxes, the later ones by simpler palmette finials.

Of far greater significance was the relief sculpture which was
used architecturally. Monumental stone sculpture and architecture began in Greece at about the same time and owned the
same source of inspiration. The two arts were always closely
associated, and we read of several architects who also enjoyed
reputations in sculpture and other arts. To use actual figure
sculptures as architectural members was a practice met in the
Near East rather than Egypt. It was never very popular in
Greece. The obvious exceptions are the well-known caryatids
of the Erechtheion in Athens, and these are anticipated in the
Archaic period in the girls who stood in place of columns in
the porches of treasuries at Delphi. The Greek practice was to
apply sculpture to those parts of a building which invited it
but never to let the sculpture dominate the architecture, as
could happen in the Near East and Egypt. In practice this
meant only sanctuary buildings in the Archaic period. On
Ionic temples there could be relief sculpture in friezes along
the top of the walls or over the colonnades; on Doric temples
in the triangular pediments and in the rectangular metopes of
the entablature over the columns. Figures in the round might
crown the gable top and corners.

124

So that figures could be seen at a distance somewhat deeper relief was admitted for temple sculpture, but even so it was still very shallow for some of the bold, overlapping compositions which the Archaic sculptor attempted. The rectangular metope panels were generally decorated with two-figure compositions – a fight or the like, and the action was only rarely allowed to carry over from one metope to the next, across the dividing upright (triglyph). Some of the earliest metopes, like that from the Sicyonian building at Delphi, are also the most intricate; but sculptors came to realize that simplicity was more effective. For friezes, on the other hand, where the spectator was obliged to observe carefully the development of the action and the role of each individual figure, far more ambitious scenes were attempted. Another of the small buildings at Delphi, the Siphnian Treasury, provides the best examples of this period. On one long side the battle of the gods and giants is related. The relief is quite high, and the artist makes good use of it to suggest the depth and mass of the struggling figures. This is often done by bringing details of the remoter figures in the composition into the front plane of the carving. In the illustration [74] two giants are seen striding off to the left. Herakles, his lion-skin knotted at his

74. Frieze: battle of gods and giants. About 525 B.C.

neck, supports the goddess Cybele in her chariot (the wheels would have been added as a separate piece) and her lions join in the fight. At the right the divine twins Apollo and Artemis continued the action. The groups of combatants allow the eye to take in at a glance the individual encounters, but do not interrupt the over-all flow of the action. This is no easy feat, and the full measure of the Greeks' success in this sort of narrative art can be appreciated when it is compared with the more episodic treatment of relief friezes in Assyria or Egypt. Indeed the Siphnian reliefs are distinguished from these purely narrative reliefs in the same way that Homer's text is distinguished from a mere chronicle of events.

The stone buildings of Egypt had inspired the evolution in Greece of regular orders of stone architecture. These served as the basic structural and decorative units of the only important buildings on which the Greeks were prepared to lavish time and money – their temples. Central Greece and the Peloponnese were the home of the Doric order. This presents some forms and mouldings which are reminiscent of Egypt, but for the most part Doric architecture is a sophisticated version in stone of the sort of timberwork which went before; not a straight translation, but a formal composition of various timber and brick forms, not all of them relevant to the position they occupy in the stone order. It is an austere order. The columns have no separate bases but grow straight from the temple floor. The capitals are round cushions beneath a square abacus. Above comes the smooth architrave, binding together the colonnades; then the rhythm of triglyphs and – often sculptured – metopes, below the gabled roof. Archaic Doric columns, with their heavy proportions, cigar-shaped outlines and bulging capitals are reassuring in their stolidity [75] but this was never to be the order with which to express an architecture of delicacy and space.

The Ionic order, which was evolved in the islands and Ionia, admits even less of Egypt, beyond the basic idea of the stone order for the columns and upper works. There is also, in contrast with the Doric, a far greater variety in the decorative forms of capital and base, and a concern with superficial detail and elegance which we have found characteristic of the sculpture of the same region. The inspiration for the main parts of the Ionic order seems to lie in the floral and volute motifs found on minor works in the Near East, especially on furniture. Rings of leaves, as of a palm, commonly appear as finials

75. Temple of Apollo at Corinth. About 550 B.C.

for legs of chairs or tables, or on smaller works, like ivory fly-whisks. There are a few examples of the same motif in Near Eastern stone pillar bases, but the Greeks adapted it for use as a column capital, with overlapping leaves and lotuses on a bell-shaped core. They also experimented with a version of the Egyptian palm capital. Later, in the sixth century, volutes springing from a ring of leaves at the top of the shaft formed the so-called Aeolic, or Proto-ionic capital, another form common in minor Near Eastern work, where the volutes can be seen to be stylizations of the overhanging leaves of a palm tree. The upper works of the immense temples designed by Ionian Greeks at Samos and Ephesus demanded columns with broader bearing surfaces. The volutes of the capital are pulled apart to lie flat, like a cushion with rolled sides, and eventually are joined to make the canonic Ionic capitals. The ring of leaves below has become the simple egg-and-dart moulding, and there is sometimes a floral necking on the shaft [76]. The columns have disk bases, turned like wooden furniture, and their shafts carry many sharp flutes, unlike the Doric shafts which have no bases and fewer flutes. Only later

127

76. Ionic capital. About 500 B.C.

do Ionic columns have the characteristic flattened ridges between the flutes. The upper works of an Ionic building are
composed of continuous friezes, articulated only horizontally,
without the panels of the Doric triglyph and metope system.
Within this order infinite variety was introduced by individual
architects and schools, even in neighbouring islands. Sculpture was admitted to the drums of column bases at Ephesus
and Didyma; on Samos the columns wore fine floral neckings
[76], a fashion recalled in the Erechtheion in Athens; on
Chios the canonic egg-and-dart and related mouldings were
translated into floral friezes, and on occasion colossal lion's
paws were used as the bases for the ends of walls (*antae*) –
another motif taken from furniture and enlarged to fit (rather
unhappily) a building. Other elegant versions of Ionic ornament in stone can be seen in the volute and floral patterns
which decorated furniture or minor structures, like altars or
thrones, and in the decorative finials for tombstones. The best
of these, on Samos, carry delicately carved leaves, alternately
concave and convex, or all concave [as in 77]. The type was
one which Athens was quick to copy.

   The one thing that both Doric and Ionic temples shared, at
least in basic outline, was their ground plan, determined by the
history of Greek temple building and by their function.
Temples were houses for a deity, whose cult image stood or
sat in a large hall, facing through the main door towards the
altar outside, generally in the east. Before the door was a

128

77. Gravestone capital. About 530 B.C.

78. Warrior and old man. About 540 B.C. (Bronze)

porch. This '*cella*' and porch is the nucleus of the temple, but
it is the columns in the porch, and the colonnades surrounding
the whole structure, which give Greek temples their characteristic appearance. They make them more than simple shelters
for a statue – the visible expression of a city's piety and wealth.
In acquiring their monumental form in stone the temples not
only became the focus for worship, but they also physically
dominated any city, for there were no other buildings of
comparable size, no palaces as we know them, and only later
any large civic offices, law courts or shops. In this early period
the contrast between the monumental marble buildings for
the gods and the mud-brick houses of the citizenry must have
been extraordinary. The temples did not invite the spectator
to enter. Their religious and artistic effect was achieved by
their simple presence. Divine protection was made manifest to
everyone, and was expressed in architecture whose massive-
ness guaranteed its permanence and bore witness to the power
of the god it housed.

The Archaic artist's achievement in these two major arts, architecture and sculpture, set the pattern for the evolution of the full Classical style in the fifth century. If vase painting has occupied us longer, this is because more of it survives to study, and because it mirrors accurately both the development of other arts and the regional differences in the Greek world. There are other miscalled 'minor' arts too which cannot be ignored (minor only for their size or the scant evidence which remains). Only at the end of the Archaic period do we begin to find life-size bronze statues, but small bronze statuettes had always been popular. Generally they follow very closely the conventions of major sculpture in proportions and detail. Probably the most important of such small bronzes are those designed as decorative attachments to vases or as the handles of mirrors. On bronze vases they may appear in the round set on the rims or at the handles, and the larger vessels also have relief figures in friezes around their necks. The figures are cast individually, never more than one from one mould, and finished with the burin or chisel and by polishing. A fine pair is shown here [78], a warrior and an old man. They are from Olympia and probably stood on the rim of a cauldron. The centaur [79], was a similar fitting. Clay figures were more carefully reproduced from moulds, but there are some among

79. Centaur. 525–500 B.C. (Bronze)

80. Plaque: griffin. About 550 B.C. (Gold)

the legion which have been found in sanctuaries and tombs which carry something of the finesse of the larger works.

The gold and ivory for jewellery and seals or statuettes appear to have been in short supply in the sixth century, by comparison with the riches in these materials of the seventh century. Some gold plaques at Delphi seem East Greek work [80]. In gem engraving, on the other hand, the artist adopted new materials and new techniques to good effect. The earlier stone seals – the island gems described in the last chapter – were cut free-hand in comparatively soft stone. In the sixth century harder stones, both local (like rock crystal) and imported (like carnelian and chalcedony) came into use, especially in the eastern Greek states which were in closer touch with Phoenicia and the sources of the stones. The popular shape was the scarab, with its back cut in the form of a beetle in the Egyptian manner, set in a swivel hoop so that the engraved base could be twisted outwards when required for sealing. The cutting in harder stones was now done with the help of a cutting wheel, a technique which had been forgotten in Greece since the Bronze Age. This made it easier to give volume to the bodies and limbs of the figures. Details were still cut free-hand, and the amazing precision exercised by the artist loses nothing in magnification under a modern lens – an aid such as the artist himself probably never enjoyed. The oval field to be carved presented the same sort of problems as did the *tondi* within cups, and animals [81a] or crouching and kneeling figures are most common on the small stones.

The techniques of gem-cutting were the same as those employed for the cutting of metal dies for coins. Greeks began to mint silver coins in any numbers only in the sixth century, and the earliest dies are cut in styles quite close to the island gems. Later, the deeper cutting and detail of the scarabs is seen also in the coin dies, together with masterful compositions in the circle, which recall the cup painters [81b]. And the miniature masterpieces of the die-engraver were mass produced, to pass from hand to hand and be more widely admired than any original works in gold or semi-precious stones.

Thus far we have looked only at the manner of Archaic Greek art. In every sphere it has been characterized by precision, from the monumental works of sculpture and architecture, to the miniatures in stone and bronze and the drawing

a. Gemstone:
Chimaera.
About 630 B.C.

b. Silver coin of
Naxos in Sicily:
head of Dionysos
and a satyr.
About 470 B.C.

on clay vases. This is native to all Greek art in all periods and must be related to (if not in part occasioned by) the rigours of technique – the cutting of hard stone for both statues and gems, the engraving of bronze, the uncompromising linear styles of vase painting. Nothing is left to the imagination, but every line, stroke and plane is explicit and complete, expressing all that the artist wished to convey about his subject within the limitations of his material and technique. But in Greek art content is as important as manner. The artist's preoccupation with portrayal of a human body reflects an attitude which is eminent in Greek life and thought. The subjects, mortal or divine, which the artist shows bear witness not only to his interests but to the whole society of which he was a member. The Greek saw his gods in human form and the Olympian family is distinguished from an Athenian family in art only by their attributes: the Greek poet attributed to his gods all human frailties of judgement and passion: and the deepest religious thought of the Greeks is best appreciated in the work of philosophers whose study was man and his intelligence. In concentrating on the representation of the perfect male body the Greek artist was affirming his confidence in the divinity of man. Whether this derived from or led to the Greeks' open approval of male homosexuality is a difficult question to answer.

Although so much of the major art of the Archaic period was devoted to religious ends it is still not true to say that any distinct religious art, in the real sense of the term, was developed. The national and local sanctuaries of the Greeks were the great display grounds for the arts of their day and of earlier times. State vied with state in the architectural elegance of the pavilions or treasuries which they built in them, and even the building of the god's own temple was at times a matter for the display of outside patronage rather than the sanctuary's own resources. Here too stood the votive monuments, which generally took the form of statuary, commemorating successes in war or the games, the success both of states and of individuals. The minor offerings too, jewellery, ivory, statuettes, find their place in the colonnades and storerooms of the god's precinct. It must have been collections of this sort, from all parts of the Greek world, which contributed to the astonishing unity and even development of the arts in all parts of Greece in the Archaic period and later. But the offerings seldom bore any direct reference to the deity. The *korai* were dedicated as permanent attendants to the shrine. Statues of the god might be offered, but in poses that reminded the viewer of some of his exploits or displayed his attributes – Zeus hurling his thunderbolt, the armed Athena. Even on the temples themselves the decorative sculpture need have no immediate reference to the god housed within, or even represent him; subjects were generally chosen from current mythological favourites, sometimes with regard for local legend.

One new way in which the artists came to treat the gods may serve to illustrate this difference between worship and art. Homer and the epic poets had presented the gods as an Olympian family, subject to the internal rivalries, weaknesses and alliances of any mortal home. This artificial, literary conception was strictly at variance with Greek practice in worship, for each state had its patron deity, here Zeus, there Apollo, who was expected to exercise all divine functions as well as those more specifically attributed to him. Other gods might be worshipped by his side, for their particular services, but there was no question yet of organized worship of the Olympians as a family. Seventh-century Greek art is true to this, showing the gods in their individual exploits, or occasionally in their traditional pairs – Artemis and Apollo, Ares and Aphrodite, Zeus and Hera. From the second quarter of the sixth century onwards they are shown as the Homeric family. They sit together as a family group, presided over by Zeus. There they argue and gesticulate, setting a pattern, it may be, for the counsels of the new near-democracies of Greece. They fight together now. The great war of the gods and giants suddenly becomes popular, and the regiment of gods is shown fighting in concert. Dionysos traps his adversary in a vine, Hephaestus hurls burning coals, Zeus wields his bolt, Poseidon grasps his trident, Athena her spear. We see Hephaestus in action [82] with Poseidon (also heaving part of an island) and Hermes. Even farce is admitted to Olympus. When Hephaestus angered Hera she threw him out, and down to earth. But he had fixed her throne so that when she sat on it she could not get up. The gods could not persuade the crippled Hephaestus to return and release her until Dionysos, with the rout of satyrs, made the god drunk and led him back. The return of Hephaestus, the anxious gods and immobile Hera fill a frieze on the François Vase which is perhaps the most famous and informative of all black-figure vases with its many scenes and over two hundred figures. All these are the new themes which

82. Athenian red-figure cup: gods fighting giants. By the Brygos Painter. About 490 B.C.

became popular with both vase painters and sculptors (like the assembly and fight with the giants on the Siphnian Treasury [74]). But this is no religious art, for the situations are as contrived as they are in Homer, and it might well be that their popularity was occasioned by a definitive edition of the poet's (or poets') works. Many have thought that such an edition was made in sixth-century Athens: it is in Athenian art that most of the new scenes appear: and it is in Athens (in 522) that an altar is first set up to the Twelve Gods, as a group or family.

By no means all the narrative scenes in Archaic art – be they on vases, bronze plaques or stone relief – deal with the Olympian gods and their exploits. Most, indeed, are devoted to the activities of the heroes, some of them minor divinities, others the protagonists in the epic poems. In the sixth century Herakles was far and away the most popular. He represented the triumph of sheer physical and mortal strength over the powers of darkness, though not without some divine assistance and a fair measure of cunning. Literally hundreds of vases have survived showing his struggle against the Nemean lion, and his other labours and adventures are well documented by the artists. His encounter with the deer is shown here [83] on a '*mastos*' cup, shaped like a breast. The canonic twelve labours as we know them in Classical and Roman art have not yet been determined (it took the fifth-century sculpture at

83. Athenian black-figure *mastos*: Herakles and stag. About 510 B.C.

Olympia to begin to standardize the Herakles cycle) and there are plenty of minor stories, some of them owning no surviving version in literature whatsoever. Even so, for these and other scenes a clear, although not rigid iconography soon grew up, in some ways comparable with that of Early Christian art. For example, there was an extremely limited number of ways in which the vase-painter would show Herakles' encounter with the lion – grappling it standing or kneeling, or throwing it like a wrestler. Painters could vary their treatment of the stock themes by introducing other figures. It was at any rate normal practice to fill in around the central group with nameless on-lookers who play no part in the action. Individuals also had their conventional dress by which they could be recognized: Herakles had club and lion skin, Hermes his *caduceus* and winged boots. Sometimes identification was assisted by in-scriptions written beside the figures, and there were times when this display of literacy was *de rigueur*, and the less gifted wrote mock inscriptions to satisfy the unlettered or the un-Greek. On some vases, the inscriptions themselves can form an important part of the pattern.

Another licence allowed the artist was the abbreviation of some stock groups, or omission of figures: thus Perseus can run away without pursuers, a Gorgon chase without a quarry, or Paris judge without the full complement of goddesses (although, in the Archaic period, Paris is usually shown in full flight from his judicial responsibilities).

The moment chosen for illustration is almost always that in which the principal action takes place: the lion is being throttled, the Minotaur stabbed, with the action moving from left to right, victors on the spectators' left. This direct, un-subtle narrative of an heroic action is in keeping with what we can judge of the Archaic spirit, but in later times more sensitive artists chose less expected moments to portray, before or after the main action. There are intimations of this feeling in the sixth century – as in Exekias' famous vase where Ajax is shown contemplating suicide, planting his sword upright in the ground, and not in the usual style, already impaled. Some of the quieter scenes with heroes arming, or returning from a journey, are in the same vein. On the vase of which a detail is shown here [84] the greatest of the Athenian black-figure painters, Exekias again, shows the home-coming of the Dios-curi, Kastor and Polydeukes (Pollux). Their father Tyndareus strokes the horse's muzzle while a lad brings out a stool, a

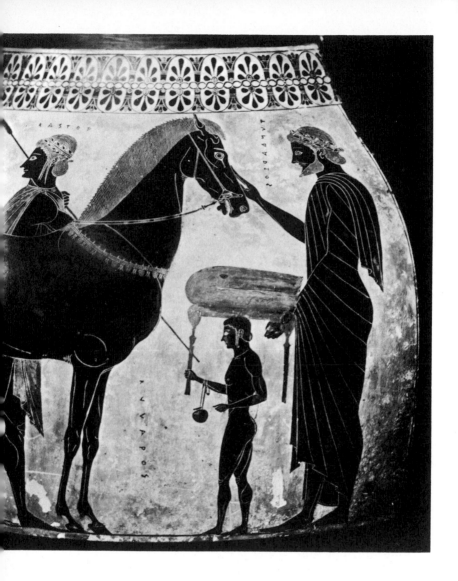

4. Athenian black-figure vase detail: return of Dioscuri. By Exekias. About 540 B.C.

change of clothing and an oil flask (for the bath and rub-down) for the heroes. The names are painted by the figures, and without them we might take this for an ordinary mortal home-coming.

Emotion or mood is expressed by action and not by facial expression. We set so much store by the success with which a painter shows the character or mood of his subject that it is hard to envisage a time in which these considerations meant nothing to an artist. The most that we may see, and that rarely, is a furrowed brow or lips drawn back from teeth in

85. Head of a wind-demon. About 570 B.C.

agony. Old age can be characterized by white hair; old women are more portly, young girls short and slim; a beard marks the passing of adolescence. Only in caricatures or grotesque heads, of satyrs or monsters, do we sometimes catch a suggestion of expression, beyond the purely horrific. A head of the triple wind-monster who looked at the spectator from a temple on the Athenian Acropolis [85] has a bland, though somewhat menacing air. And, of course, there is no individual portraiture, although in details, especially of sculpture, the artist does seem to be making generalized portraits by showing individual

86. Gravestone fragment: boxer. About 550 B.C.

characteristics (an obvious example is the boxer's puffed features and ears on a gravestone [86]). All this has to be borne in mind before too much is made of the idealization of heads in the Classical period. The setting, too, is generally left unspecified, or conveyed by figures. There is no interest in landscape, and where we do find the rare vase scene in which the trees or a vine are in nearly the right proportion to the adjacent figures the indirect influence of Egyptian painting may be suspected.

Apart from the purely mythological scenes there is a growing number of representations of everyday life, showing the artist looking for subjects in what went on around him at the same time as he was taking a more serious interest in accurate portrayal of the human figure. Beside the simple story-telling, as by puppets, we have for the first time in Greece an art which could reflect accurately contemporary life and habits. Here again, however, we find that there are soon developed a number of stock scenes – the return or departure of a warrior, a procession of guests bearing gifts to a newly married couple, the ritual mourning at the laying-out of the dead – as well as a host of individual studies which tell us much more about both domestic life and trade. Some of the genre scenes are played by divine actors as often as mortals, and here again we see the Greek characteristically finding no less of interest in everyday mortal scenes than in divine. Perhaps this is a feature of any self-possessed and self-confident society and art. Rarely, there may be reflections of a contemporary event as in the scenes of women chatting at a fountain house which appear at the time when the Athenian tyrants were reorganizing the city water supply. When so many vessels were destined for drinking parties, work in the vineyard, and indeed the parties themselves [87], were naturally popular subjects. Athletics provided a host of motifs – youths wrestling, running, jumping. In the palaestra and training ground [88] the artist found

87. (Left) Athenian red-figure cup detail: flautist and dancer. By Epiktetos.
About 510 B.C.

88. Athenian red-figure calyx *crater*: athletes. By Euphronios. About 500 B.C.

the subjects and poses which stimulated his interest in representing the human body at rest or in motion, and obliged him to rise above the limitations of his technique to make the most of his subjects.

Not only do these scenes tell us much about details of contemporary life, but the very choice of subjects should also reveal what, to the artist, seemed either the most characteristic or, from his point of view, the most worthwhile themes. It is perhaps dangerous to generalize too freely about the nature of a society from its representational art alone, but in this instance we are helped by literary evidence too. So many subjects deal with wholly feminine pursuits – weaving, gossip at the fountain – that there can be no question here of a society in which women are kept wholly in the background, which is the impression we get from Near Eastern decorative art in most periods. On the other hand we are spared the cloying boudoir scenes of later Classical art. Women are still far from their pedestal. The work of slaves too was not considered an unsuitable theme. In what must already have been quite a liberal society the artist was free to look beyond the worlds of myth, fantasy or wealth for his subjects.

It must, however, be admitted that some artists could turn just as readily to subjects which many would consider gross. The frankness of many of the scenes shocks an age which still prefers to draw a veil before the obvious pleasures of the bed and table, which prefers the salacious hint to explicit statement. In the sixth century (and to a lesser extent later) Greek artists – including the finest – depict love-making in all its variety as freely as they might some epic encounter, while courting scenes between men and youths soon acquire a clearly defined iconographic tradition of their own. In the same way all the pleasures of the drinking party and cabaret are displayed, from the formal toast to the party games and the squalid consequences of over-drinking. Yet all these do not mean that this was an age of undue licence or prurience, nor should we blame the artist for any obsession with the improper. The earliest extant painted decoration for a Greek temple (at Thermon) includes a scene of love-making. In every street and before houses stood herms, pillars topped with a head of Hermes and with an erect phallus at the front: sacred objects of cult, intended to ward off evil. There may be some element of magic and much that seems primitive in all this, but there was no place for false prudery when the organs and act of generation were exposed in this way. We may compare the sacred relief sculptures of India, and contrast the way that the Romans and others have preferred to keep such matters under cover.

This is the place to consider the Greek satyr, who was born and reached maturity in the Archaic period. He has a shaggy head, a horse's ears, tail and sometimes legs, and displays aggressive virility: more the artist's creation than the literary man's, and he owns no obvious mythical background, though he looks something like an abbreviated centaur. As a spirit of the wild and of generally abandoned behaviour he is naturally attracted to the god of wine, Dionysos, and consorts with the god's maenads – wild women whose function and origin is far more serious and deeply religious [89]. For the wilder dances of mortal *komasts* the satyr's costume is soon adopted, and thus, under Dionysos' patronage, the satyr plays his part in the development of the Greek theatre. But in his behaviour and origins he seems no more than a projection of the ordinary man's desires to let convention go hang, to run wild and enjoy life, wine, women and all, to the full capacity of his belly. His first century of life is his best, for later he is tamed, to do tricks and even lead a normal family life. But in the Archaic period he leers hopefully at the maenads, works hard

89. Athenian red-figure cup detail: satyrs and maenad. By Oltos. About 520 B.C.

90. Athenian black-figure vase: Dionysos, satyrs and maenad at vintage.
By the Amasis Painter. About 550 B.C.

90. Athenian black-figure vase: Dionysos, satyrs and maenad at vintage.
By the Amasis Painter. About 550 B.C.

for his master at worth-while jobs like the vintage [90], and provides many of the rare moments of humour and emotion in Greek art of these years. And to judge from the frequency of scenes he is something of a sportsman, for he seems to relish the pursuit at least as much as the consummation. This is the atmosphere of Keats's lines –

> What men or gods are these? What maidens loth?
> What mad pursuit? What struggle to escape?
> What pipes and timbrels? What wild ecstasy?

– but his 'Grecian Urn' was a vase of very different type and period.

If we turn from this art of narrative, action and the simplest genre subjects, to the poets of the day, and especially to the lyric poets from Sappho to Anacreon, we can find points of comparison enough but there is still a significant gulf between them. The poets made full use of myth as well as everyday situations, but they could use a story more subtly – to point a moral, to express an emotion – and they were able to convey a depth of compassion which far outstripped the ambition and ability of contemporary painters and sculptors. Archaic Greek art appeals to a sense of beauty (however we may define it), even to a sense of the dramatic; it makes but slight demands on the essentially human emotions.

Of the artists in Athens we know that some were rich enough to commission their colleagues to execute dedications for them; more than one relief or statue base on the Athenian Acropolis shows this. On many vases young notables (rarely girls) are praised for their looks by inscriptions – '*Leagros kalos*', Leagros is beautiful. It has been argued that this shows some familiarity with high society, but the vases so inscribed were not made for circulation only among the upper set, and they reflect no more upon the status of the inscriber than do the numerous tributes to members of the royal family or popular entertainers which now appear on trivial articles of everyday use or even clothing.

We also come closer to the artists as individuals in the Archaic period since enough of their work has been preserved and studied to enable us to distinguish personalities. It was surely a self-conscious pride rather than desire for advertisement that led artists to begin signing their works. By the mid seventh century we find some signatures on vases. They use the Greek word 'made' (*epoiesen*). It is usually assumed that they refer to painter and not potter, but in Chios at the end of the century such a signature (of Nikesermos) appears on an otherwise undecorated cup. In the sixth century the painter may distinguish his function by saying 'painted' (*egrapsen*). The simple 'made' (*epoiesen*) can sometimes be shown to refer to the potter, since by now there was a real and justifiable pride in the craft, but it could still certainly be used by a painter, and may on occasion refer to the owner of the workshop. In early days painter and potter (and pottery-owner) would normally be one and the same man. Even in sixth-century Athens this must have remained the norm. The first clear sign of specialization is on the famous François Vase, painted about 570 B.C., signed by both potter and painter, and closer study of painting and pottery styles shows that it became more common in the red-figure period. But it should be remarked that signatures of any sort are the exception, not the rule, and most of the finest painters have had to be renamed by modern scholars.

Stone sculpture was promoted from being a decorative craft when the challenges of size and material were accepted in the second half of the seventh century. A sculptor required to inscribe the dedicator's name on a statue or its base would easily be moved to add his own signature. By about 600 we find a sculptor of Naxos dedicating one of his own works on Delos. Sculptors often name their own town or island when they sign their names. Inscribed bases found in the main sanctuaries as well as the references of ancient authors show how widely they travelled, either seeking commissions or at the invitation of states and individuals. We hear of sculptors who were architects, and one (Theodorus of Samos) who was a gem-engraver too. Vase painters might well have been the artists who worked also on plastered walls or wooden panels. In Etruria the hand of one Greek artist is seen by some in the figures on certain vases and tomb paintings. Families of artists too are recorded. From the monuments themselves we find an Athenian sculptor (Pollias), with a distinguished vase-painter son, Euthymides, who painted a fine clay plaque for him to dedicate on the Acropolis, where his statues already stood.

If the individual artist can now be recognized more clearly, so too can the hallmarks of a school. Here we are faced with a problem which deserves a digression since it illustrates neatly the way in which artists may have travelled and artistic principles have been transplanted in an age of considerable invention and experiment. It concerns the Ionians of East Greece, their influence on the other states of Greece whose works we have already considered, and their influence on peoples outside the Greek world to whom the last two chapters of this book are devoted.

During the sixth century life for the East Greeks was uneasy and dangerous, balanced between short periods of high prosperity and threats of imminent destruction. Smyrna was sacked by the Lydians early in the century, and in the mid century, when Lydia in its turn fell to the Persians, the newcomers from the east dealt no less harshly with several of the Greek cities and islands. Artists, perhaps, travel more readily than most professional folk, but these were years in which families or whole townships might prefer to try their fortune overseas rather than face the threat of barbarians who were easily aroused by Greek independence and impudence. Where could they go? Clearly the islands and Attica would beckon for their proximity and kinship. Farther off, the Black Sea was already ringed with Ionian colonies growing fat on the cornlands by the great rivers, from the Danube to the Don, and on the fisheries. In Egypt the Greek trading town at Naucratis was largely an East Greek venture and would invite tradesmen and craftsmen. In the west too there were Ionian colonies. The Phocaeans had founded Marseille in 600, and when their mother city was faced with destruction at the hands of the Persians, the inhabitants moved west to settle in Corsica and join other Greek colonies. The Milesians had been counselled to evacuate to Sardinia. Ionian skippers were well acquainted with the western seas and would find homes there for their kin.

We look now for evidence of the work of emigrant artists from East Greece. In the islands and Athens it is clear enough, for statue bases signed by Ionian artists have been found. The *kore* type, with the *chiton* [72], was probably introduced by the mid century from East Greece rather than the islands, although this could be disputed. About 530 B.C. Athens begins to use Ionic capitals for the *kore* dedications on columns, and also adopts the Ionian palmette finial [77] for gravestones. At just this time red-figure is invented for vases, and who can say what part may have been taken by artists used to a tradition in which outline drawing had never wholly given place to black-figure?

In the Black Sea the situation is clearer. The colonies, colonists and artists are Ionian, whatever their motives might have been for going there, and the metalwork which they executed for the Scythians (see chapter 6) is wholly Ionian in style, or tempered with elements of the Scythian animal style such as were in fact also met in Ionia, at Ephesus [104].

In Egypt, at Naucratis, Chian potters had opened a workshop for producing votive pottery before the middle of the century, and vase-painters from North Ionia (perhaps Clazomenae) and Rhodes also seem to have practised their craft in Egypt in the second half of the century. This is shown by the distribution of their wares and some of the motifs painted on them.

In the west, Ionian artists found homes in what was one of the most lively markets for Greek art – Etruria – rather than in the Greek colonies. The latter, by now, had either developed artistic traditions of their own or preferred to ape and buy homeland styles. Even so, in the late Archaic period their stone architecture admits a number of Ionic features which are not matched in the Ionic of East Greece or in that of, for example, Athens. In Etruria artists from one North Ionian workshop of black-figure vase painters, whose work has been found in the Black Sea colonies and in Egypt, set to work producing the so-called 'Northampton Group' vases and 'Campana dinoi'. Later, another artist settled in Caere and made a series of finely painted water-jars for the local market. All these wares were lively and colourful, conceding something, inevitably, to dominant Athenian fashions in black-figure, but wholly distinctive and Ionian in their character. Probably for this very reason they were short-lived. Etruscan taste in painted pottery had been completely conditioned by Athenian vases, and the only workshop started by Ionians which succeeded, and eventually attracted and trained Etruscan painters, was the one that made most concessions in vase-shape, style and some subjects, to what Etruscans had grown used to from Athens. This produced the so-called Pontic vases [94]. What is Athenian in them is there because of the market they served. What is Ionian can only be there because Ionian artists put it there.

Vase painting is not the best medium for demonstrating the work of Ionians in Etruria at this time, once Athenian standards for vases were so dominant, but there are other, more cogent indications of their presence. Etruscan clay revetments for buildings copy closely a type which had been developed in East Greece, and which is clearly distinguishable from those of both mainland Greece and the western Greek colonies. In stone sculpture the animals (the lion has been the subject of a special study recently) exhibit traits which can derive only from East Greece. We cannot point to imported models, so we must suppose immigrant artists and teachers. The same is true of minor works in bronze, some of which copy Ionian forms extremely closely. Stone reliefs for tomb monuments are close to the vases in style and occasionally admit subjects more familiar from Athenian vases, but have nothing Athenian in their style, nor can their characteristics be derived from earlier Etruscan, Orientalizing art. Tomb paintings of the mid century vividly recall East Greek outline-drawing on vases, and work by Greek hands in Phrygia. A new class of gold and silver rings appears in the middle of the sixth century. They bear devices which are close to the vases we have noticed, and are of a shape (Egyptian in origin) which in the Greek world had hitherto only been copied in East Greece. The earliest gems – carnelian scarabs – cut in Etruria towards the end of the century, follow the devices and style of East Greek gems as much as those of the islands or central Greece. And we may add here those workshops in which, it seems, East Greek artists worked beside Phoenicians to make jasper scarabs both in the west (many have been found in Carthage, Ibiza and Sardinia) and in the east (in Syria and Phoenicia itself).

The cumulative effect of all this evidence is impressive. It shows how in special circumstances artists and ideas could pass from one part of the Greek world to another, carrying on old traditions or inspiring new ones. The way that the Ionian artists left their mark so clearly and in so many different ways is the more remarkable because in most places the finest and most popular work was that produced by Athens and the centres of homeland Greece rather than in the East Greek areas.

Politics are hardly involved in the story of Archaic Greek art. The Greek states set up monuments as offerings to the gods – statuary or treasuries, either at home or in the national sanctuaries – to celebrate victories, but beyond a modest inscription there is nothing to distinguish these dedications from others made for non-political occasions. The choice of a particular myth may sometimes seem deliberate. It has been suggested, for instance, that a statuary group showing Herakles seizing Apollo's tripod was a distinct reference to the First Sacred War over Delphi. Certainly, the later popularity and setting of scenes showing Greeks defeating Amazons or centaurs appear as a comment on contemporary Greek successes against the barbarians in the field. On a different plane Athenian artists saw to it that the Athenian Theseus challenged Herakles for the position of being the most popular hero – at least in the art of Athens – and he even took over the iconography of some of Herakles' labours. This was a matter of local patriotism with a distinctly political flavour.

The courts of the tyrants, especially those of Samos and Athens, provided liberal patronage for artists, poets and musicians, but the temples and public works which they designed served the community as much as they enhanced the reputation of the temporal leaders. The citizens of Sparta were supposed to have led a traditionally austere life, but in the Archaic period their studios produced as fine and as lively works of art as any in Greece, and they enjoyed a special reputation for their metalwork. The workshops may not have been manned by full citizens, but their products bear a distinctive character which can only be called Spartan, and although there was also a brisk trade in them, they seem to have been primarily for local use.

The Archaic period ends, or rather gives way to the Classical – for we must not imagine any abrupt transition – in the first half of the fifth century. In 479 B.C. the Greeks finally repulsed the Persians from their shores, and in the west their compatriots in Sicily had, for a while at least, stayed the power of Carthage. Faced with the threat of the barbarian the Greeks – or most of them – could forget internal differences and unite in defence. In it they realized more fully the basic unity of their way of life, thought and art, and if internal dissensions were again to break out, even more violently, they were never to forget the success of their stand as a nation united in purpose as in speech.

The mortal dangers and military successes mark an important point in the political history of Greece. There is no particular reason why they should also mark an important transition in the history of her art, and yet it seems that they do. It is not easy to see just why this should be so, but there is in fifth-century art a calm and confidence in both expression and technique, which contrasts strangely with the nervous fussy energy of Archaic art. But it was in the sixth century and the earlier, Orientalizing period, that the foundations were laid for all that was achieved in Classical Greece. The sculptors of the late Archaic period were already beginning to break

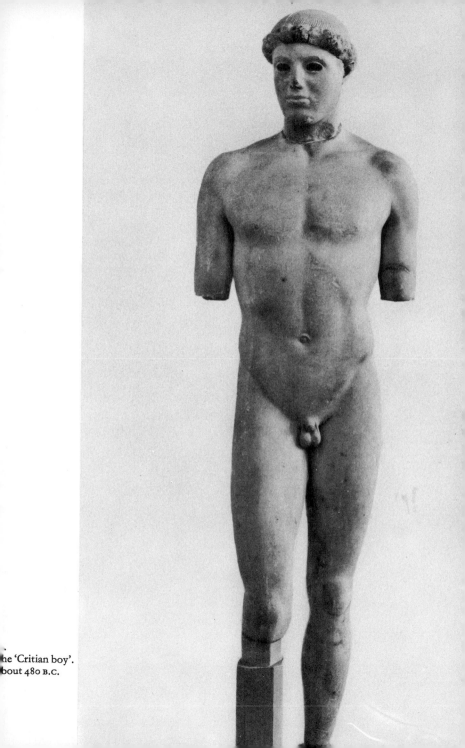

The 'Critian boy'.
About 480 B.C.

with the formality of the *kouros* pose, and to show accurately that subtle shift in the balance of standing figures [91] which gave the breath of life to what was still a highly mannered form. In architecture the main orders were already established and it was a matter now of further refinement of details and proportions. The main changes were to be in the Ionic order, the development of which lay now in Athenian rather than East Greek hands. In vase painting the new red-figure technique had already reached its prime, and the only innovations in this or a cognate art were to be in major painting on panels or walls. The feeling for monumental art and pure pattern, and the qualities of precision were there still to inform the work, as they had been in the Geometric period, but in the intervening two centuries the exciting influence of the foreigners' arts and the prolific invention of Greek artists had transformed the content and appearance of Greek art into that which we call Classical.

5

The Etruscans

The art of Etruria has attracted far more attention than it deserves, and it earns a place in this book less for its intrinsic merit or its contribution to the history of western art, than for the revealing contrast it affords to the achievements of the Greeks, and for the way it shows what the effect of Greek art could be on a relatively primitive people. Rome, of course, inherited the Greek tradition, making the link between ancient Greece and the modern world, and Rome in its early days shared in the general culture of Etruria. But although Roman art does owe something to what may be distinguished as peculiarly Etruscan – notably in the development of portraiture – still the greatest influence in the Roman world was that of the Greeks themselves.

Since our purpose is also to use Etruscan art to illustrate one of the means by which Greek art was transmitted to the barbarians (the writer and his readers are included here), it will be convenient to consider first how Etruscan art evolved from virtually nothing in the Greek Orientalizing period and then to see how thoroughly Greek art and Greek artists could work upon the sensibilities of the 'conditioned' native artists. We have already had occasion to remark (p. 150 ff.) the profound effect of one group of immigrant artists in the sixth century.

The Etruscans themselves were not indigenous to Italy. It seems likely that they arrived there quite early in the Greek Iron Age from Asia Minor. They brought little enough of the material culture of the east with them, and shared rather in the great Bronze Age culture of the Italian peninsula. When we are first able to recognize them as a major power in Italy they appear in a loosely knit confederation of fortified cities. Their country, west of the Apennines, was rich in timber and minerals, which must have been their main source of prosperity. It is not clear how early the Etruscans also became a naval power, rivalling the Greeks and Phoenicians (from Carthage) in the west.

In the middle of the eighth century B.C. the earliest Greek colonies in the west were founded on the doorstep of the Etruscans, on the island of Ischia, and at Cumae on the mainland opposite. They were in part the result of Greek interest in the mineral wealth of Etruria, and in part they fostered that interest, but they had also to help provide land and sustenance for a population already outgrowing the shores of Greece and her islands. At all events, the foundation of these and other Greek colonies in south Italy and Sicily marks the beginning of the import into Etruria of Greek pottery and other objects. At precisely the same time Etruria received oriental works, especially bronzes. These may have been brought by Phoenicians who were also active in the west Mediterranean, but might as well have been carried by Greeks, since in these years they had no luxury goods of their own to offer, and it was the same Greeks (Euboeans) who had opened up the eastern markets and who settled the earliest western colonies. From this amalgam of eastern and Greek influences Etruscan art emerged.

The effect of eastern art on the Etruscans was very different from its effect on the Greeks. First, the Etruscans had no strong existing artistic tradition like the Greek Geometric; secondly, they were temperamentally quite unlike the Greeks. The first objects of Greco-oriental appearance (for early Etruscan art is no more than this) were almost certainly made by Greeks in the west, either in the Greek cities or in Etruria itself: clay vases, native in their shapes, but carrying the more banal types of Greek Geometric decoration. Quite soon local artists must have started making similar works, and they are followed by imitations of the Corinthian animal frieze vases in black-figure. On these the individuality of the Etruscan artist was expressed in some odd distortions of the animals, and a fondness for the more grisly motifs – lions with limbs and torsos hanging from their jaws – or for the more exotic monsters. Beside them too we see decorative details which are copied from eastern works, and these offer patterns unfamiliar on Greek vases.

The Etruscans were far less critical than the Greeks in accepting and copying oriental forms and techniques. This is most readily seen in metalwork. Several fine oriental or strongly Orientalizing bronzes reached Etruria in the later eighth and seventh centuries, and we may be sure that, as in Greece, artists trained in the new techniques also taught their craft there. Etruscan resources of bronze and iron meant that her metalworkers were on the whole more prolific than their Greek contemporaries, and there was soon a flood of hammered bronzes decorated with a mixture of Greek and oriental patterns worked in repoussé. Perhaps the most spectacular effect of this oriental influence in metalwork is the remarkable gold jewellery which was made in Etruria in the seventh century. Many of the forms of safety-pins (*fibulae*), or bracelets, copy Italian types, but they are executed with extreme care and elaboration, and show the technique of filigree completely mastered. Moreover gold granulation is used to render figures in outline or silhouette in a way never met in Greece. This is not the only original feature in Etruscan gold-work of these years, and if it seems to us vulgar and flamboyant it can still be admired for the excellence and precision of its technique.

Gold and ivory are materials which attracted the best craftsmen in the Orientalizing periods of both Greece and Etruria, but Etruscan ivories, like their gold, are far more eastern in appearance and subject than the Greek. In this Etruscan seventh-century art faithfully mirrors its sources – the east for techniques in metal and precious material, Greece for vase-painting and much decorative ornament. The Etruscans were uncritical enthusiasts in what they made or what they had made for them. They found themselves the focus of attention in the western Mediterranean because of their material resources and acquired a taste for luxury as soon as they had the riches with which to satisfy it. But although they were wealthy and had the artistic abilities of Greece and the east thrust upon them, they could not in their own art achieve greatness.

The lack of any native artistic tradition, and, it seems, of the sort of character that can absorb instruction and still produce vital original work, made Etruscan artists singularly vulnerable to the influence of any more active or more enlightened schools. After the Orientalizing period the sixth century shows Etruscan art dominated by Greek influence. This was twofold.

First there was the influence of the western Greeks, the immediate neighbours of the Etruscans. The Greek colonies in south Italy and Sicily had grown considerably in the seventh and sixth centuries, and many of the cities were at least the equals in wealth of the major city states of Greece. The art of the western Greeks is largely an extension of that of the homeland, but it has a character of its own as well. Lacking fine white marble, its sculpture was comparatively uninspired and generally conservative beside that of, say, Athens or the Peloponnese. Clay became rather more widely used for sculpture, and especially for the decoration of the upper works of buildings. Stone architecture was bold, imaginative and ambitious, combining rather sophisticated versions of the Doric order with projects on a scale worthy of some Ionian tyrant. For decorated pottery the western Greeks were generally satisfied with wares imported from Corinth or Athens, but there were a few local schools in the seventh century, and in the sixth a distinguished one set up by Chalcidian artists [65]. There were also several distinctive schools producing minor works in clay and bronze. In general western Greek work tends to be rather mechanical and occasionally florid. The Etruscans traded freely with the Greek colonies in Italy and Sicily, when they were not fighting them, and some features of sixth-century Etruscan art – as in bronze-work – can be traced directly to western Greek influence, rather than to anything produced in Greece itself.

The second main source of influence in Etruria was that of immigrant artists, largely, it seems, from the East Greek cities. Of these something has been said already. At present our concern is to examine the degree of hellenization of Etruscan art in the full Archaic period.

The Etruscans are probably best known and best remembered for their decorated tombs. These offer a rich series of paintings, the like of which are not to be found in Greece, for the simple reason that the Greeks did not build tombs of this type and their wall paintings in other buildings have inevitably perished. The earliest Etruscan tomb paintings are on clay plaques [92], later on the plastered walls [93]. Their style at first is Orientalizing and Archaic Greek, as is most of their subject-matter. Some are very closely related to a group of vases which were painted by a Greek in Etruria towards the end of the sixth century. The figures are very much like those on vases, but of course more colour could be used and there is no black-figure incision. From the mid sixth century on, their style suggests that East Greek hands or teachers were at work. It was in East Greece that outline styles of drawing had lingered, and there are close parallels on wall paintings discovered in Phrygia (at Gordium), which were certainly painted by Ionians. But in Etruria there are also several which are the work of Etruscan artists, betrayed by their naïve misunderstanding

92. Etruscan plaque from a tomb wall. 550–525 B.C. (Clay)

93. Tomba dei Tori painting: Achilles ambushes Troilos. About 530 B.C.

of Greek subjects, or by some quite un-Greek styles in decoration, including landscape. The Etruscans never quite shook off the example of the east and Egypt, kept alive, it may be, by their relations with the Phoenicians and Carthage. An example of the Etruscan treatment of a Greek theme is shown here [93]; the conventional Greek scene of Achilles ambushing Troilos at a fountain has been crammed with superfluous architecture and foliage, and Achilles, who should be the dominant figure, is reduced in scale and lost in the shrubbery.

In vase-painting the Etruscan versions of Corinthian animal frieze vases were long popular, but there was a lively trade in vases from Greece, and some potters made lines especially for the Etruscan market. Immigrant East Greek artists set up small workshops in Etruria at and after the middle of the sixth century, and a new series of Etruscan black-figure vases began, very largely inspired by East Greek artists, it seems, but with a distinct though superficial Athenian look, since this was what Etruscan taste had come to approve. The vases are called 'Pontic' – one of the many misnomers which are current in classical archaeology, the result of scholarly speculation in earlier years. The old animal friezes are still in evidence, but they are executed in a lively, colourful style, and the figure scenes include some original interpretations of Greek myth. In our illustration [94] we see part of a Judgement of Paris, the prince ignored by his cattle while he greets the goddesses being led to him on the other side of the vase. And on a later vase [95] the artist has taken the Greek eyes motif and added the serpents to suggest the brows, nose and mouth of a grinning mask. But the Etruscan vases lose their Greek air of competence and in the hands of native artists become trite and uninteresting.

Like the western Greeks, the Etruscans had no marble for statuary. Their gaunt funerary lions and sphinxes are carved from soft tufa, and the same material was used for the relief decoration of funeral urns (of Chiusi) which carry figures similar to those of Pontic vases or the tomb paintings. Clay was more widely used, even for figures of more than life size, and in this material the Etruscans achieved work of no little merit. The clay statuary was often used for architectural decoration (the famous Apollo of Veii was one of several figures which strode along the ridge of a high roof) and it appears on the lids of clay sarcophagi, like the famous group

94. 'Pontic' vase detail: Paris and herd. About 540 B.C.

95. Etruscan black-figure vase. About 500 B.C.

96. Group from a sarcophagus. About 520 B.C. (Clay)

from Caere, in Rome [96]. In their other clay revetments, often carrying lively relief scenes, the Etruscans are again following a western Greek practice, although not the western Greek style.

The ready availability of metals encouraged the bronze-smiths to produce works which in size and occasionally in quality can compare well with those of the Greeks themselves. Special types of tripod and candelabrum were evolved from western Greek patterns, and the statuettes which adorned these and other bronze vessels capture much of the fresh precision of Archaic Greek work, adding a coarse vigour which is only Etruscan. Part of the fittings of an Etruscan bronze tripod is shown here [97], decorated with a group of a lion attacking a bull, executed in a lively but more mannered style than contemporary Greek work.

For gem-engraving the Etruscans were wholly in the hands of the Greeks. Some carnelian scarabs from Greece reached Etruria in the sixth century, and soon local workshops were established by Greeks for similar stones, usually set in swivel rings of gold. Etruscan artists followed the Greek lead. They copied the subjects of the Greek gems, adding a few less common ones (as they did on the vases). Characteristically

97. Tripod fitting: lion and bull. 525–500 B.C. (Bronze)

98. Pendant: satyr's head. About 500 B.C. (Gold)

the Etruscans gave their gems a brilliant polish, and, unlike the Greeks, lavished as much care on the beetle-back as on the intaglio. Gold rings, of a shape met in Egypt and Phoenicia and with figures like those on the Pontic vases, were also introduced by the East Greeks, and superb filigree gold jewellery was still made [98]. This intense production of *objets de luxe* went on at the same time as a brisk trade in commonplace, not to say shoddy, goods: a marked contrast with Greece where there was perhaps a more limited production of luxury goods, but where the high quality of Archaic Greek work informs even the humblest clay figurine.

The subjects chosen by the Etruscan artists were not wholly determined by their Greek models. They display an almost obsessive preoccupation with death and with gruesome themes of demons or dismemberment. Their scenes of gaiety seem almost calculated in their abandon beside the simple objective way in which the Greek artist could treat what pleased him or others. The finest objects in Greece come to us from the temple sanctuaries, in Etruria from the cemeteries, and this concern with the tomb casts a pall over Etruscan art.

But their love of colour was uninhibited and unsubtle. It lends a vulgar gaiety to their paintings. Their love of caricature and the grotesque may have led to a less idealistic approach to portraiture than that of the Greeks. We can judge how the Greeks summed up their taste by the vases which were made deliberately for the Etruscan market, with old-fashioned animal friezes, banal repetitive figure scenes, gory myths and wantonness in as much colour as black-figure allowed. In view of this we should be grateful that the Greeks also sent some of their finest vases to Etruria, where they have survived better

99. Incised mirror back: satyr and maenad. About 460 B.C. (Bronze)

than they would have done in Greek cemeteries, houses or sanctuaries.

While some of the features we have described were peculiarly Etruscan, there is still virtually nothing in this art which is truly original, nothing which is not to some degree derived from eastern or Greek art. When the source of inspiration for gem-engraving, for instance, was removed, that craft soon degenerated, and the Archaic forms survived unchanged for some two centuries. At the end of the Archaic period and after it the best artists were good copyists: the incised mirror in London [99] is a very good approximation to Greek work of the latest Archaic style, as we know it from the vases.

The later stages of Etruscan art, of the Classical and hellenistic periods, are virtually provincial Greek. This is the point at which to recall that Rome in her early years shared this culture; that the Republic which grew strong enough to absorb Etruria and eventually the western Greeks was a society whose art was Greek in character, learned in the first place by Etruscans in the seventh and sixth centuries, fostered by the example and works of the Greeks and their colonists. 'Roman art' is what the Romans added to the tradition in which they had been reared. But this is a story for another book.

6

The Scythians

In a volume which sets out to survey the pre-classical art of western Europe the record of Greece and the Aegean islands inevitably takes pride of place. The older civilizations of the Near East and Egypt also play their part, but their contribution was made, not by the imposition of their arts and ideals, but, as we have seen, by the deliberate and discriminate choice of the Greeks themselves. All these foreigners, with their incomprehensible tongues, were 'barbarians' to the Greeks, who were becoming increasingly aware of their bond of language and of the qualities which distinguished them from the rest of the known world. Indeed they were soon to be able to resist successfully the armed challenge of the greatest of the eastern empires, the Persian. There were other encounters with the barbarians who played their part in the history of Greek art and of its contribution to the west. We have seen already something of the effect of the Greeks on artless barbarians, like the Etruscans, but there was also a very different sort of encounter with a more sophisticated race, the Scythians. It was an abortive one, so far as the history of Greek art is concerned, but it introduced a totally different artistic tradition, arising from a fundamentally different racial character, history and religion, in its way illustrating concisely that deep-rooted opposition between the north and south which is a basic factor in all aspects of European culture. Successors to this new tradition are to have a profound effect on western art in periods later than that discussed in this book. Here we have to observe the results of a first attempt to compromise between the formal but essentially human arts of the Mediterranean and the vivid, discursive decoration of peoples who had roamed the frozen steppes of Asia.

The art of the northern nomads is often referred to as the 'animal style'. In sharp contrast with the formal, disciplined, representational arts of Mesopotamia or Greece it is essentially decorative. Patterns based on the bodies or members of animals are developed as required over any given shape, object or area. The general effect is abstract rather than realistic, curvilinear rather than architectonic; and it is essentially two-dimensional. But despite the stylization, despite the multiplicity of spirals and tangled ornaments which are the result of the artists' peculiar treatment of his natural themes, this is still an art of live forms and not of mere abstractions. The animals persist in being alive even when most ruthlessly schematized. The measure of the difference from Greek art is immense and unbridgeable. Think how some of the Orientalizing animals of Greece are reduced to pure patterns of limbs and anatomical features, at once more realistic but less real than the nomad 'animal style'; how their abstractions are geometric in form, often rectilinear, and never space-filling, unpredictable arabesques. Little wonder that Greek artists were impressed by what they saw, but baffled in their attempt to imitate.

The 'animal style' owns no single home, but it can be recognized from end to end of Europe and Asia at different periods ranging over more than two thousand years. We associate it especially with the nomad peoples of the steppes, which stretch from Manchuria to the Black Sea. In the Far East the arts of the nomads had a profound effect on the development of Chinese art from a very early date. In the Near East the metalworking cultures of Persia in the second and early first millennia B.C. acknowledge its style. To the north we think first of the Scythians who occupied the grasslands of South Russia and the Caucasus in the first millennium B.C. It was from them that the Greek artists first learned something of the animal style, in their colonies on the cold northern shores of the Black Sea.

The Royal Scythians – to distinguish them from their less venturesome kinsfolk – had broken in upon the kingdoms of the Near East in the seventh century B.C., but were eventually evicted by the Medes at the end of the century. Through their contacts with the urban civilizations of Mesopotamia they no doubt lost some of the characteristics of their nomadic culture. Certainly, their art had assimilated much from the more formal arts of Assyria and Persia, and this is well shown in the royal treasure of Sakiz. The same style, or rather the same mixture of styles, since the art of the nomads never combined successfully with any other, appears in objects found in the rich Scythian graves near the northern and eastern shores of the Black Sea. These mark the return of the Royal Scythians to the north, and their occupation of the rich South Russian grasslands. While the way of life of the main population in these areas was probably still shifting, nomadic, the groups of the great tombs show that movement was probably now more limited, and it is not long before there is evidence for settled courts, towns and kingdoms. This was a process hastened by the example of the Greeks, whose towns set a pattern for urban life, and whose commercial interests promised a revenue which settled farmers would enjoy better than nomads.

The first Greek colonies on the north shores of the Black Sea were founded towards the end of the seventh century on or near the mouths of the great rivers, and in the east of the Crimea opposite some of the earlier groups of Royal Scythian tombs. They had been attracted there by the rich cornland and the fisheries, and were arriving on these shores at about the time that the Royal Scythians were moving into the adjacent areas, after their martial irruption into the Near East and subsequent withdrawal. The Greeks came from Ionian Miletus for the most part, and the arts they practised were in the developed Orientalizing style then current in all Greek lands. The Scythians' art was that uneasy mixture of the Near East and the nomad animal style which we have already mentioned, and in their tombs we find examples of it alongside Greek vases which are the first indication of the newcomers from the Aegean.

The Ionian cities traded with the Scythians, bought the corn grown on the farmlands which they controlled, and admitted them to their cities. They were dealing with a more civilized and, in their arts, a more mature people than the Etruscans. Clearly the Greeks were none too sure what to make of them. The Scythians were 'dead set against foreign ways, especially against Greek ways', says Herodotus, and he tells how a Scythian prince who set up in a rich town house in one of the Greek cities and took to Dionysiac orgies was despised and killed by his kin. The Scythians were magnificent archers and horsemen, qualities which recommended them as mercenaries to the Greeks. In the fifth century Athens recruited them for her metropolitan police, but the Scythian bobby in Aristophanes' *Ecclesiazusae* is portrayed as a lewd blockhead. The average Greek probably thought of this milk-drinking people as no more than a source for slaves.

The Greek artists, however, who lived and worked in the Black Sea colonies, were faced with the problems of satisfying the exotic tastes of their rich neighbours. Their own Orientalizing art still had much in common with the Near Eastern, Assyrian elements in Scythian art, but was no more easily reconciled with the animal style. The earliest Greek works which seem to have been made by Ionian artists especially for the Scythians – often objects of native Scythian form and all found in the Scythian tombs – simply juxtapose the two styles. Thus, the gilt silver mirror from a Kelermes tomb carries ordinary Greek Orientalizing figures of a recumbent animal in the pure animal style [100]. The only other concessions are a bear and the introduction of a scene showing the Arimasps fighting a griffin, since this was an encounter set by the Greeks in the distant frozen north. But for these the style and iconography are Greek, since narrative played no part in Scythian art.

Later Greco-Scythian work attempted to weld the styles more effectively. Ionian artists would find nothing alien in an art which sought to cover by a multiplicity of patterns whatever surface or shape was offered. But whereas the nomads did this by developing a single motif or organically adding to it, the Greeks sought the same effect by adding an assortment of figures and groups, not closely interrelated. At the same time the free curves which are so characteristic of the animal style are subjected to Greek discipline. Losing their fluidity they also lose their effect. The result is well shown in the gold appliqué relief of a stag [101]. Its pose and the reduplication of the horn motif ending with an animal head (a ram) is in the spirit of the animal style, but mechanical in execution. The neat, Greek figures of a griffin, hare, lion and dog, are simply attached to the creature and do not grow from it as they do on the wholly Scythian lion [102], on which miniatures of the whole creature decorate the tail and replace the knobbed feet and claws.

The failure to reconcile the two art forms was recognized in the early fifth century, and from then on such work as the Greeks did for the Scythians was done in a wholly Greek style, conceding only to its sponsors in subject-matter and shape. Independently, and in centres further removed from the immediate and overpowering influence of the Ionian cities, the animal style lived on [103]. It developed hardly at all, being a fully sufficient and satisfying idiom in itself. Its influence was never felt in the Aegean in antiquity, and the stray northern object which penetrated so far, like the small

00. Mirror back. 600–575 B.C. (Gilt silver)

101. Stag with repoussé animals. 500–475 B.C. (Gold)

102. Lion. 600–500 B.C. (Gold)

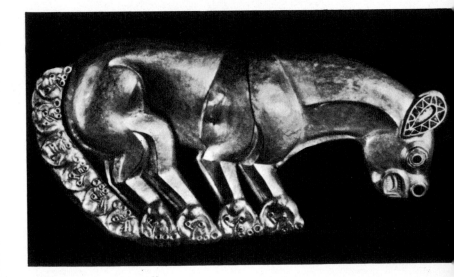

103. Horse attacked by lion. 500–400 B.C. (Gold)

104. Boar. 600–500 B.C. (Ivory)

ivory boar [104] found at Ephesus, stands out as wholly alien in an Archaic Greek assemblage of votive objects. Outside and on the borders of the Greek and then the Roman world in Europe the native crafts of La Tène, of the Celts, owed much to the animal-style arts of the eastern steppes. The strength of tradition, surviving through to the Sutton Hoo treasure in England or the Book of Kells, emerges much more clearly when it is looked at beside the quite different, Classical discipline of the Mediterranean countries. The two had nothing in common and never really combined or compromised. Both played their part in the development of western art in later centuries, and although it is the Classical tradition which was foremost in the arts of the Renaissance, it would be wrong to forget the contribution made by that other, totally opposed style, and the occasion on which it first met and attempted to come to terms with the art and artists of Greece.

Catalogue of Illustrations

1. FIGURE OF A WOMAN. About 3000 B.C. Clay. 18·2 cms.(Photograph, J. L. Caskey.)
   From Lerna, near Argos
2. FIGURE OF A WOMAN. About 3000 B.C. Marble. 76·2 cms. *Oxford, Ashmolean Museum* AE. 176. (Photograph, Museum.)
   From Amorgos
3. BEAKED JUG. About 1700 B.C. 27 cms. *Heraklion Museum.* (Photograph, Museum.)
   From Phaistos, Crete
4. IMPRESSIONS OF SEALS. 1700–1600 B.C. Widths 1·7, 2·1, 2·1 cms. *Oxford, Ashmolean Museum* 1938: 793, 964, 955. A and B. Unknown provenance; C. From Knossos, Crete
   A. A jasper prism with cats' heads. B. An agate, flattened cylinder with a bull drinking at a tank and a youth leaping on to its neck
   C. A chalcedony, flattened cylinder with acrobats in a field of lilies
5. WORSHIPPER OR 'FLUTE-PLAYER'. 1700–1600 B.C. Bronze. 14 cms. *Leiden, Rijksmuseum* B.147.
6. FIGURE OF A WOMAN. 1700–1600 B.C. Bronze. 19 cms. *Berlin, Staatliche Museen* 8092. (Photograph, Museum.)
7. TWO JUGS. About 2000 B.C. Veined marble. 7·2, 12 cms.*Heraklion Museum.* (Photograph, Hirmer.)
   From Mochlos, East Crete
8. PENDANT. 1700–1600 B.C. 6 cms. *London, British Museum* BMCJ 762. (Photograph, Museum.)
   Part of the 'Aegina Treasure', but probably from Mallia, Crete. Showing a prince on a boat, with two geese, and 'horns'
9. PENDANT. 1700–1600 B.C. Gold. Width 4·7 cms. *Heraklion Museum.* (Photograph, Xylouris.)
   From near Mallia, Crete. Two hornets
10. MINIATURE FRESCO. 1700–1600 B.C. Restored copy of fragments in *Heraklion Museum.* (Photograph, Ashmolean Museum.)
    From Knossos, Crete
11. BEAKED JUG WITH GRASSES. 1600–1500 B.C. 29 cms. *Heraklion Museum.* (Photograph, Hirmer.)
    From Phaistos, Crete
12. OCTOPUS FLASK. About 1500 B.C. 28 cms. *Heraklion Museum.* (Photograph, Hirmer.)
    From Palaikastro, East Crete
13. THE HARVESTERS' VASE (RHYTON). 1600–1500 B.C. Black steatite. Width 11·5 cms. *Heraklion Museum.* (Photograph, Hirmer.)
    From Hagia Triada, Crete

14. IMPRESSIONS OF SEALS. 1500–1400 B.C. Widths, 2·2, 2 cms. *Oxford, Ashmolean Museum* 1938: 1041, 1058. A. An agate lentoid with a monster and a bull. B. A rock crystal lentoid with a contorted lion
15. FRESCO WITH PARTRIDGES. About 1500 B.C. Restored copy of fragments in *Heraklion Museum*. (Photograph, Ashmolean Museum.)
From the 'Caravanserai', Knossos, Crete
16. CUP: THE CAPTURE OF BULLS. About 1500 B.C. Gold. 7·8 cms. *Athens, National Museum*. (Photograph, German Archaeological Institute, Athens.)
From Vaphio, near Sparta
17. CUP: OCTOPUSES. About 1500 B.C. Gold. Width 17·3 cms. *Athens, National Museum*. (Photograph, Hirmer.)
From Midea, near Argos
18. BULL'S HEAD (RHYTON). About 1500 B.C. Steatite. *Heraklion Museum*. (Photograph, Sansoni.)
19. DAGGER BLADE: CATS HUNTING DUCKS. About 1500 B.C. Bronze inlaid with silver, gold and *niello*. *Athens, National Museum*. (Photograph, Hirmer.)
From a Shaft Grave, Mycenae
20. DISK. About 1500 B.C. Gold. 6 cms. *Athens, National Museum*.
From a Shaft Grave, Mycenae
21. RING: STAG HUNT. About 1500 B.C. Gold. Width 3 cms. *Athens, National Museum*. (Photograph, German Archaeological Institute, Athens.)
From a Shaft Grave, Mycenae
22. PALACE-STYLE JAR. About 1400 B.C. 70 cms. *Heraklion Museum*. (Photograph, Museum.)
From Knossos, Crete
23. JAR WITH AXES. About 1400 B.C. *Heraklion Museum*. (Photograph, Sansoni.)
From Knossos, Crete. Much restored
24. ALABASTRON: GRIFFINS AND YOUNG. About 1200 B.C. *Chalcis Museum*. (Photograph, M. R. Popham.)
From Lefkandi, Euboea. Found in 1964
25. TWO WOMEN AND A CHILD. About 1400 B.C. Ivory. 7·8 cms. *Athens, National Museum*. (Photograph, Hirmer.)
From Mycenae
26. THE LION GATE AT MYCENAE. About 1250 B.C. (Photograph, Hirmer.)
27. THE TOMB 'TREASURY OF ATREUS', MYCENAE. 1300–1250 B.C.
28. ATHENIAN PROTOGEOMETRIC VASE. About 950 B.C. 52 cms. *Athens, Kerameikos Museum*. (Photograph, German Archaeological Institute, Athens.)
From the Kerameikos Cemetery, Athens
29. ATHENIAN GEOMETRIC JUG. About 750 B.C. 33·3 cms. *Tübingen, Archaeological Institute* 2657. (Photograph, Museum.)
30. ATHENIAN GEOMETRIC VASE DETAIL: FUNERAL BIER AND MOURNERS. About 750 B.C. *Athens, National Museum* 804.
31. ATHENIAN GEOMETRIC CUP: LION CHASING DEER. About 700 B.C. *Athens, Vlasto Collection*.
32. ATHENIAN GEOMETRIC JUG DETAIL: SHIPWRECK. About 750 B.C. *Munich, Museum antiker Kleinkunst*. (Photograph, Museum.)
33. FIGURE OF A MAN. About 750 B.C. Bronze. 14·4 cms. *Olympia Museum* B 4600. (Photograph, German Archaeological Institute, Athens.)
From Olympia.

34. HEAD OF A MAN. About 700 B.C. Clay. 11·5 cms. *Sparta Museum*. (Photograph, German Archaeological Institute, Athens.)
From Amyklai, near Sparta

35. HELMET-MAKER. About 700 B.C. Bronze. 5·2 cms. *New York, Metropolitan Museum* 42.11.42, Fletcher Fund, 1942. (Photograph, Museum.)

36. HERO FIGHTING A CENTAUR. About 750 B.C. Bronze. 11 cms. *New York, Metropolitan Museum* 17. 190. 2072, given by J. Pierpont Morgan, 1917. (Photograph, Museum.)

37. HORSE. About 750 B.C. Bronze. 16 cms. *Berlin, Staatliche Museen* 31317. (Photograph, Museum.)

38. FIBULA SAFETY-PIN: STAG. About 700 B.C. Gold. *London, British Museum* 1960. 11–1.46. (Photograph, Museum.)
Probably from Attica

39. IMPRESSION OF A SEAL: BOWMAN AND CENTAUR. About 700 B.C. Stone. 2·2 × 2 cms. *Paris, Bibliothèque Nationale* M 5837.

40. PROTOCORINTHIAN ALABASTRON: TWO STAGS. About 640 B.C. 6·9 cms. *Tübingen, Archaeological Institute*. (Photograph, Museum.)

41. PROTOCORINTHIAN CLAY BOX, BASE. About 700 B.C. 28 cms. *Athens, National Museum*. (After Payne, *Protokorinthische Vasenmalerei*, pl.8,1.)
From the Heraeum near Argos

42. GRIFFIN'S HEAD. About 650 B.C. Bronze. 27·8 cms. *Olympia Museum* B 145. (Photograph, German Archaeological Institute, Athens.)
From Olympia. From an attachment to a cauldron

43. FIGURE OF A GIRL. About 750 B.C. Ivory. 24 cms. *Athens, National Museum* 776. (Photograph, German Archaeological Institute, Athens.)
From the Kerameikos Cemetery, Athens

44. PROTOCORINTHIAN JUG. About 730 B.C. 21·6 cms. *London, British Museum* 59. 2–16.38. (Photograph, Museum.)

45. PROTOCORINTHIAN FLASK (ARYBALLOS). About 660 B.C. 7·4 cms. *Boston, Museum of Fine Arts* 95.12. (Photograph, Museum.)

46. PROTOCORINTHIAN CUP FRAGMENT: CHIMAERA. About 660 B.C. *Aegina Museum*. (Photograph, German Archaeological Institute, Athens.)
From Aegina

47. PROTOCORINTHIAN 'CHIGI VASE' DETAIL: HORSEMEN. About 650 B.C. *Rome, Villa Giulia Museum*. (Photograph, Hirmer.)
From Veii, Etruria

48. PLAQUE: KAINEUS BEATEN INTO THE GROUND BY CENTAURS. About 600 B.C. Bronze. 22·5 cms. *Olympia Museum*. (Photograph, German Archaeological Institute, Athens.)
From Olympia

49. PROTO-ATTIC LID: HORSES AND FOAL. By the Analatos Painter. About 700 B.C. 25·8 cms. *London, British Museum* O.C. 385. (Photograph, Museum.)

50. PROTO-ATTIC VASE DETAIL: ODYSSEUS BLINDING POLYPHEMUS. About 650 B.C. *Eleusis Museum*. (After Mylonas, *Protoattic Amphora*, pl.8.)
From Eleusis. Found in 1954

51. GRIFFIN JUG. About 650 B.C. 41·2 cms. *London, British Museum* 73.8–20. 385. (Photograph, Museum.)
From Aegina

52. ISLAND VASE FRAGMENT: ARTEMIS AND A LION. About 600 B.C. 25 cms. *Berlin, Staatliche Museen* 301. (Photograph, Museum.)

53. RELIEF VASE DETAIL: PERSEUS DECAPITATES THE HORSE-MEDUSA. About 630 B.C. *Paris, Louvre* Ca 795.

54. PLAQUE: HUNTER AND GOAT. 650–625 B.C. Bronze. 9·7 cms. *Oxford, Ashmolean Museum.* G 438. (Photograph [negative print], Museum.)
From the Dictaean Cave, Crete

55. RHODIAN VASE. About 600 B.C. 31 cms. *London, British Museum* 61.10–24. 14. (Photograph, Museum.)

56. CASTS OF STATUES OF WOMEN. A. The Auxerre goddess. About 625 B.C. Limestone. 65 cms. *Paris, Louvre*; B. Dedication by Nicandre on Delos. About 625 B.C. Marble. 1·75 m. *Athens, National Museum.* (Photograph, Ashmolean Museum Cast Gallery.)

57. ATTIC KOUROS. About 600 B.C. Marble. 1·84 m. *New York, Metropolitan Museum* 32.11.1, Fletcher Fund, 1932. (Photograph, Museum.)

58. KOUROS. About 620 B.C. Bronze. 19·7 cms. *Athens, National Museum.* (Photograph, German Archaeological Institute, Athens.)
From Delphi

59. PLAQUES: ARTEMIS WITH LIONS. About 625 B.C. Gold. 6 cms. *London, British Museum* BMCJ 1128. (Photograph, Museum.)
From Camirus, Rhodes

60. EAR-RING PENDANT: GRIFFIN HEADS. About 625 B.C. Gold. 6 cms. *Berlin, Staatliche Museen* G 141. (Photograph, Museum.)
From Melos

61. KNEELING YOUTH. 625–600 B.C. Ivory. 14·5 cms. *Samos Museum.* (Photograph, German Archaeological Institute, Athens.)
From Samos. Once attached to a lyre (?)

62. IMPRESSIONS OF SEALS. A. Ivory disk with a flying bird. About 650 B.C. 4·8 cms. *Athens, National Museum.* (Photograph, German Archaeological Institute, Athens.)
From the Heraeum near Argos
B. Stone amygdaloid with a bull. About 600 B.C. Width 3 cms.

63. ATHENIAN BLACK-FIGURE VASE DETAIL: GRIFFIN. By the Nessos Painter. About 620 B.C. *Berlin, Staatliche Museen* 1961.7. (Photograph, Museum.)

64. ATHENIAN BLACK-FIGURE JUG: LION. By the Gorgon Painter. About 590 B.C. *Kassel, Hessisches Landesmuseum* T 669. (Photograph, Museum.)

65. CHALCIDIAN CUP: EYES AND A MAENAD. By the Phineus Painter. About 530 B.C. *New York, Metropolitan Museum* 98.8.25, given by F. W. Rhinelander, 1898. (Photograph, Museum.)

66. ATHENIAN WHITE-GROUND CUP FRAGMENT: TRITON. By the Eleusis Painter. About 500 B.C. *Eleusis Museum.*

67. ATHENIAN RED-FIGURE CUP DETAIL: YOUTH AND RABBIT. By the Berlin Painter. About 490 B.C. *Athens, Agora Museum* P 24113. (Photograph, Museum.)
From the Agora, Athens

68. ATHENIAN RED-FIGURE CUP: FLUTE-GIRL WITH WINE JAR. About 510 B.C. Width 42·7 cms. *New York, Metropolitan Museum* 56.171. 61, Fletcher Fund, 1956. (Photograph, Museum.)

69. KOUROS. About 550 B.C. Marble. 1·53 m. *Munich, Glyptothek* 168. (Photograph, Hirmer.)
From Tenea near Corinth

70. KOUROS HEAD. About 530 B.C. Marble. *Athens, National Museum.* (Photograph, German Archaeological Institute, Athens.)
From Anavyssos, near Athens

71. HEAD OF ATHENA. About 490 B.C. Clay. 22·4 cms. *Olympia Museum* T 6. (Photograph, German Archaeological Institute, Athens.) From Olympia

72. KORE. About 510 B.C. Marble. *Athens, Acropolis Museum* 675. (Photograph, Museum.)

73. GRAVESTONE FRAGMENT: YOUTH WITH DISCUS. About 550 B.C. Marble. 34 cms. *Athens, National Museum* 38. From the Dipylon Cemetery, Athens

74. FRIEZE: BATTLE OF GODS AND GIANTS. About 525 B.C. Marble. 64 cms. *Delphi Museum.* (Photograph, A. Frantz.) From the Siphnian Treasury, Delphi

75. TEMPLE OF APOLLO AT CORINTH. About 550 B.C. (Photograph, Hirmer.)

76. IONIC CAPITAL. About 500 B.C. Marble. Width *c.* 3 m. *Samos Heraeum Museum.* (Drawing, Gruben.)

77. GRAVESTONE CAPITAL. About 530 B.C. Marble. 42 cms. *Samos Museum.* (Photograph, German Archaeological Institute, Athens.) From Samos Cemetery

78. WARRIOR AND OLD MAN. About 540 B.C. Bronze. 14·3, 13·9 cms. *Olympia Museum* B 5000, B 25. (Photograph, German Archaeological Institute, Athens.) From Olympia. From the rim of a cauldron

79. CENTAUR. 525–500 B.C. Bronze. 11·5 cms. *New York, Metropolitan Museum* 17.190.2070, given by J. Pierpont Morgan. (Photograph, Museum.)

80. PLAQUE: GRIFFIN. About 550 B.C. Gold. 10 cms. *Delphi Museum.* From Delphi

81. A. GEMSTONE: CHIMAERA. About 630 B.C. Jasper. Width 1·4 cms. *London, Mrs Russell's Collection.*
B. SILVER COIN OF NAXOS IN SICILY: HEAD OF DIONYSOS AND A SATYR. About 470 B.C. (Photographs, Hirmer.)

82. ATHENIAN RED-FIGURE CUP: GODS FIGHTING GIANTS. By the Brygos Painter. About 490 B.C. Width 32 cms. *Berlin, Staatliche Museen* 2293. (Photograph, Museum.)

83. ATHENIAN BLACK-FIGURE MASTOS: HERAKLES AND STAG. About 510 B.C. *Munich, Museum antiker Kleinkunst* 2003. (Photograph, Museum.)

84. ATHENIAN BLACK-FIGURE VASE DETAIL: RETURN OF DIOSCURI. By Exekias. About 540 B.C. *Vatican Museum* 344. (Photograph, Alinari.)

85. HEAD OF A WIND-DEMON. About 570 B.C. (Photograph, Sansoni.) From the east pediment of the old Temple of Athena on the Acropolis

86. GRAVESTONE FRAGMENT: BOXER. About 550 B.C. Marble. 23 cms. *Athens, Kerameikos Museum.* (Photograph, A. Frantz.) From the Kerameikos Cemetery, Athens, found in 1953 built into the Themistoclean Wall

87. ATHENIAN RED-FIGURE CUP DETAIL: FLAUTIST AND DANCER. By Epiktetos. About 510 B.C. *London, British Museum* E 38.

88. ATHENIAN RED-FIGURE CALYX CRATER: ATHLETES. By Euphronios. About 500 B.C. 35 cms. *Berlin, Staatliche Museen* 2180. (Photograph, Museum.)

89. ATHENIAN RED-FIGURE CUP DETAIL: SATYRS AND MAENAD. By Oltos. About 520 B.C. *Copenhagen, National Museum.* (Photograph, Museum.)

90. ATHENIAN BLACK-FIGURE VASE: DIONYSOS, SATYRS AND MAENAD AT VINTAGE. By the Amasis Painter. About 550 B.C. 44 cms. *Basel, Antikenmuseum.* (Photograph, Museum.)

91. THE 'CRITIAN BOY'. About 480 B.C. Marble. 86 cms. *Athens, Acropolis Museum* 698. (Photograph, Hirmer.)

92. ETRUSCAN PLAQUE FROM A TOMB WALL. 550–525 B.C. Clay. *c.*1 m. *Paris, Louvre.*
    From Cerveteri, Etruria. A 'Campana' plaque

93. TOMBA DEI TORI PAINTING: ACHILLES AMBUSHES TROILOS. About 530 B.C.
    From Tarquinia, Etruria

94. 'PONTIC' VASE DETAIL: PARIS AND HERD. About 540 B.C. *Munich, Museum antiker Kleinkunst* 837.

95. ETRUSCAN BLACK-FIGURE VASE. About 500 B.C. *Leiden, Rijksmuseum.* (Photograph, Museum.)

96. GROUP FROM A SARCOPHAGUS. About 520 B.C. Clay. *Rome, Villa Giulia Museum.* (Photograph, Sansoni.)
    From Cerveteri, Etruria

97. TRIPOD FITTING: LION AND BULL. 525–500 B.C. Bronze. *New York, Metropolitan Museum* 60.11.11, Fletcher Fund, 1960. (Photograph, Museum.)

98. PENDANT: SATYR'S HEAD. About 500 B.C. Gold. 3·6 cms. *London, British Museum* BMCJ 1463. (Photograph, Museum.)
    From Cerveteri, Etruria

99. INCISED MIRROR BACK: SATYR AND MAENAD. About 460 B.C. Bronze. Width 15 cms. *London, Victoria and Albert Museum,* Salting Collection 707.1910. (Photograph, Museum.)

100. MIRROR BACK. 600–575 B.C. Gilt silver. *Leningrad, Hermitage.*
     From Kelermes, South Russia

101. STAG WITH REPOUSSÉ ANIMALS. 500–475 B.C. Gold. *Leningrad, Hermitage.*
     From Kul Oba, South Russia

102. LION. 600–500 B.C. Gold. *Leningrad, Hermitage.*
     From Kelermes, South Russia

103. HORSE ATTACKED BY LION. 500–400 B.C. Gold. *Leningrad, Hermitage.*

104. BOAR. 600–500 B.C. Ivory. Width 4·5 cms. *Istanbul, Archaeological Museum.* (After Akurgal, *Die Kunst Anatoliens,* fig. 185.)
     From Ephesus

The authorities and persons named are thanked for photographs and permission to reproduce them.

Books for Further Reading

Stars are awarded for the number and quality of the illustrations in each work named.

The best picturebook of prehistoric Greece which also surveys the history and society of the day is MARINATOS, S., *Crete and Mycenae**** (London, 1960). More specialist studies, but very readable, are VERMEULE, E., *Greece in the Bronze Age** (Chicago, 1964) and HUTCHINSON, R. W., *Prehistoric Crete* (Harmondsworth, 1962).

For the historical background to the Archaic period BURN, A. R., *The Lyric Age of Greece* (London, 1960) is a valuable and detailed guide. BOARDMAN, J., *The Greeks Overseas* (Harmondsworth, 1964) surveys the archaeology of colonization and trading posts while STARR, C. G., *The Origins of Greek Civilization** (New York, 1961) is a more specialist work which well combines history and archaeology. BOWRA, C. M., *The Greek Experience* (New York, 1957) is largely, but not wholly, devoted to the later period.

The early chapters of most handbooks on Greek art cover the years dealt with in this book. RICHTER, G. M. A., *Archaic Greek Art**** (Oxford, 1949) works by period and place, and her *Handbook of Greek Art*** (London, 1959) by subject, but is less reliable for the earlier period. The most useful basic handbooks are RICHTER, *Sculpture and Sculptors of the Greeks*** (Oxford, 1950) – rather dated and poor on origins; LULLIES, R., and HIRMER, M., *Greek Sculpture**** (London, 1960) – excellent commentary on individual pieces; COOK, R. M., *Greek Painted Pottery** (London, 1960) – thorough; ARIAS, P., *A History of Greek Vase-painting**** (London, 1961) – the English edition edited by Shefton is not laid out as a handbook but can serve as one; LANE, A., *Greek Pottery**** (London, 1947) – a good brief guide and reliable; ROBERTSON, C. M., *Greek Painting**** (Geneva, 1959) – excellent colour and commentary; LAWRENCE, A. W., *Greek Architecture**** (Harmondsworth, 1957); LAMB, W., *Greek and Roman Bronzes*** (London, 1929) – rather dated; HIGGINS, R. A., *Greek and Roman Jewellery*** (London, 1961). There are also monographs of special subjects or groups. For sculpture the following three books are excellently illustrated and offer full, reliable comment: PAYNE, H., and YOUNG, G. M., *Archaic Marble Sculpture from the Acropolis**** (London, 1950), RICHTER, *Kouroi**** and *The Archaic Gravestones of Attica**** (London, 1960, 1961). PAYNE, H., *Necrocorinthia*** is a specialist work on the archaic pottery of Corinth, and BEAZLEY, J. D., *The Development of Attic Black Figure** (Berkeley, 1951) a brilliant series of lectures introducing the subject. BOARDMAN, *Island Gems** (London, 1963) deals with the earlier gems.

RIIS, P. J., *An Introduction to Etruscan Art** (Copenhagen, 1953) is by far the most reliable guide, but RICHARDSON, E., *The Etruscans** (Chicago, 1964) is more up to date. Most of the other general books and nearly all the current picturebooks on Etruscan art are tendentious or unreliable. I mention only PALLOTTINO, M., *Etruscan Painting**** (Geneva, 1952) for its pictures. MINNS, E., *Scythians and Greeks** (Cambridge, 1913) is a classic, but very detailed; ROSTOVTSEFF, M., *Iranians and Greeks in South Russia* (Oxford, 1922) is shorter and more readable. RICE, T. T., *The Scythians** (London, 1957) is weakest on the period with which we deal.

Index

More about Penguins and Pelicans

If you have enjoyed reading this book you may wish to know that *Penguin Book News* appears every month. It is an attractively illustrated magazine containing a complete list of books published by Penguins and still in print, together with details of the month's new books. A specimen copy will be sent free on request.

Penguin Book News is obtainable from most bookshops; but you may prefer to become a regular subscriber at 3s. for twelve issues. Just write to Dept EP, Penguin Books Ltd, Harmondsworth, Middlesex, enclosing a cheque or postal order, and you will be put on the mailing list.

Some other books published by Penguins are described on the following pages.

Note: *Penguin Book News* is not available in the U.S.A., Canada or Australia.

Palladio

James S. Ackerman

Palladio is the most imitated architect in history. His buildings have been copied all over the Western world – from Leningrad to Philadelphia – and his ideas on proportion are still current nearly four hundred years after his death. In this, the first full account of his career to be published in English, Professor James Ackerman investigates the reasons for his enormous and enduring success. He presents him in his historical setting as the contemporary of Titian, Tintoretto, and Veronese, but is constantly alert to his relevance for us today.

The Architect and Society

The aim of this series, specially written for Penguin Books, is to present the great architects of the world in their social and cultural environments.

The Ancient World

T. R. Glover

The civilization of the Western World was born many centuries ago on the shores of the Mediterranean, and in this survey of its origins Dr Glover has reconstructed the achievements and discoveries of the Greeks and Romans. He was a scholar of great distinction who knew his sources intimately, but he reinforced his book-knowledge of the Ancient World by many prolonged journeys in these historic regions. What he has to tell us, therefore, of the growth and influence of these empires of antiquity is illuminated by his own vivid response to the environment where so much history was made. He is aware, for example, of the geographical factors which gave Troy and Babylon their significance, he can trace the strategic reasons for the imperial expansion of Persians and Assyrians, and he is no less aware of the art and literature of the Greeks and Romans than of their politics and economics. This genius for bringing the past to life is the quality, above all others, which made Dr Glover so vivid a historian, and this genius was never more brilliantly revealed than in *The Ancient World*.

Another book in the *Style and Civilization* series

Mannerism

John Shearman

The refinement of Benvenuto Cellini's golden salt cellar or the monstrous fantasies of the Boboli Gardens in Florence – both are characteristic of Mannerism, a virtuoso style of life and art that intervened between Renaissance and Baroque in the sixteenth century. Mannerism was perhaps the most self-consciously 'stylish' of all styles – in literature, music and the visual arts alike. In the way that we have once again come to appreciate *art nouveau* so it is again possible for us to understand the spirit and beauty of Mannerist art.

Style and Civilization series

Gothic

George Henderson

Notre Dame or Canterbury, exquisite illumination, stern sculpture or the stained glass of Chartres – the rich and complex nature of Gothic art has always fascinated us. Every age has held its own vision of the Gothic world – a world of barbarism, or of chivalry, or of piety. Here is an attempt to reach a deeper understanding of the Gothic style by examining its many forms in the context of contemporary religious and philosophical attitudes, and against the background of the social and political order of the Middle Ages.